© Copyright 2024 by Tenskill Mia - All rights reserved.

No part of this publication may be reproduced, distributed, or transmitted in any form or by any means, including photocopying, recording, or other electronic or mechanical methods, without the prior written permission of the publisher, except in the case of brief quotations embodied in reviews and certain other non-commercial uses permitted by copyright law.

This Book is provided with the sole purpose of providing relevant information on a specific topic for which every reasonable effort has been made to ensure that it is both accurate and reasonable. Nevertheless, by purchasing this Book you consent to the fact that the author, as well as the publisher, are in no way experts on the topics contained herein, regardless of any claims as such that may be made within. It is recommended that you always consult a professional prior to undertaking any of the advice or techniques discussed within.

Table of Contents

Introduction 8

Chapter 1: Noodles and Rice 9
- Dan Dan Noodles 10
- Hakka Noodles 11
- Garlic Noodles 12
- Singapore Noodles 13
- Chinese Birthday Noodles 14
- Glass Noodles with Napa Cabbage and Green Beans 15
- Chicken Chow Mein 16
- Beef Lo Mein 18
- Beef Chow Fun 19
- Fried Rice with Egg, Shrimp, and Scallions 20
- Spam Fried Rice 21
- Smoked Trout Fried Rice 23
- Pork Congee 24
- Steamed Rice with Bok Choy and Lap Cheung 25
- Pad See Ew 26

Chapter 2: Soups 28
- Egg Drop Soup 29
- Sizzling Rice Soup 29
- Beef Noodle Soup 30
- Hot-and-Sour Soup 32
- Watercress and Pork Soup 33
- Chinese Mushroom Soup 34
- Lotus Root with Pork Ribs Soup 35

Easy Wok Chinese Cookbook

Simple and Delicious Recipes to Steam, Sizzle, and Stir-Fry at Home.

Tenskill Mia

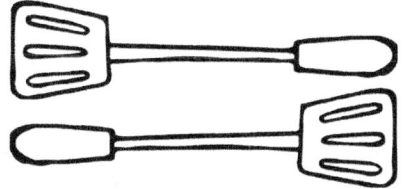

Sweet Peanut Soup 35

Wonton Soup 36

Chicken and Sweet Corn Soup 37

Chapter 3: Poultry Recipes 39

Sesame Oil Chicken 40

Orange Chicken 40

Mushroom Chicken 41

Black Pepper Chicken with Asparagus 42

Sweet and Sour Chicken 43

Chicken with Cashew Nuts 44

Honey Sesame Chicken 45

Ginger Chicken 46

Moo Goo Gai Pan 47

General Tso's Chicken 48

Chapter 4: Fish and Seafood 50

Stir-Fried Fish with Bok Choy and Ginger 51

Whole Steamed Fish with Scallions and Sizzling Ginger 52

Pepper and Salt Shrimp 53

Deep-Fried Oysters with Chili-Garlic Confetti 54

Drunken Shrimp 55

Coconut Curry Crab 56

Shanghainese-Style Stir-Fried Shrimp 57

Veggie and Seafood Stir-Fry with Crispy Rice Noodles 58

Mussels in Black Bean Sauce 59

Walnut Shrimp 60

Deep-Fried Black Pepper Squid 62

Velveted Scallops 62

Chapter 5: Pork and Beef Recipes 64

    Five-Spice Pork 65

    Pork Ribs with Black Bean Sauce 66

    Steamed Egg with Ground Pork 67

    Sichuan Twice-Cooked Pork 68

    Peking-Style Pork Ribs 69

    Pork and Mixed Vegetable Stir-Fry 70

    Moo Shu Pork Lettuce Wraps 71

    Sweet and Sour Pork 72

    Beef with Broccoli 73

    Mongolian Beef 74

    Beef with Shiitake Mushrooms 75

    Beef and Bell Pepper Stir-Fry 76

    Sichuan Beef 77

    Beef with Honey and Black Pepper Sauce 78

Chapter 6: Tofu and Vegetables 80

    Ma Po Tofu 81

    Tofu and Eggplant in Sizzling Garlic Sauce 82

    Hunan-Style Tofu 83

    Steamed Bean Curd in a Simple Sauce 84

    Stir-Fried Snow Peas 85

    Stir-Fried Spinach with Soy Sauce and Garlic 86

    Spicy Stir-Fried Napa Cabbage 86

    Stir-Fried Lettuce with Oyster Sauce 87

    Stir-Fried Bamboo Shoots and Broccoli 88

    Dry-Fried String Beans 89

Stir-Fried Mushrooms and Bok Choy 89

Stir-Fried Vegetable Medley 90

Buddha's Delight 91

Sesame Asparagus 92

Chinese Broccoli with Oyster Sauce 93

Chapter 7: Appetizers and Dim Sum Recipes 95

Chinese Chicken Salad Cups 96

Shrimp and Pork Shumai 97

Shrimp Dumplings 98

Savory Scrambled Egg and Crab Lettuce Wraps 99

Steamed Vegetable Dumplings 100

Chinese Pork Meatballs 101

Cold Sesame Noodles 102

Chapter 8: The Basics Recipes 103

Sweet and Sour Sauce 104

Basic Chinese Chicken Stock 104

Brown Sauce 105

Congee 106

Basic Sambal (Red Chili Sauce) 107

Metric Conversions 108

INTRODUCTION

The vastness of Chinese regional cuisine!
Chinese Food Quick Start - Simple and delicious stir-fry recipes that are a real crowd-pleaser.
This cookbook gives you everything you need to get started, including dozens of delicious Chinese dishes, simple instructions, troubleshooting tips and tricks, and more. From flavorful Kung Pao Chicken to crispy Sesame Beef, this authentic Chinese wok cookbook will surely wow your taste buds without blowing your budget or patience. Use the wok with confidence at home with expert advice, including a step-by-step guide to wok success.
Whether you're new to Chinese cooking or your pantry is always stocked with bean paste and chili oil, you'll find plenty of inspiration and trustworthy recipes that will become part of your family's story too.
It's time to ditch the takeout menu and start stir-frying like a seasoned chef.
Welcome to a new culinary journey through the flavors of Asia!

Chapter 1: Noodles and Rice

Dan Dan Noodles

Prep Time: 20 Minutes
Cook Time: 10 Minutes
Serves: 4

Ingredients:

- 1 teaspoon Sichuan peppercorns, toasted and ground (use less as desired)
- 1 tablespoon fermented black beans, rinsed and chopped
- 1-inch piece of fresh ginger, peeled and finely minced
- 2 small heads of baby bok choy, coarsely chopped
- ¾-pound (about 340g) thin wheat noodles
- 2 tablespoons Shaoxing rice wine, divided
- ½ cup finely chopped dry roasted peanuts
- 4-ounce (about 115g) ground pork
- 4 tablespoons vegetable oil, divided
- 2 tablespoons smooth peanut butter
- 1 tablespoon black vinegar
- 3 garlic cloves, finely minced
- 2 teaspoons light brown sugar
- 2 tablespoons Fried Chili Oil
- ¼ cup light soy sauce
- Kosher salt

Method:

1. Bring a large pot of water to a boil and cook the noodles according to package instructions. Drain and rinse with cold water and set aside.
2. Fill the pot with fresh water and bring it to a boil on the stovetop.
3. In a bowl, mix the pork with 1 tablespoon of vegetable oil, 1 tablespoon of rice wine, and a pinch of salt. Set aside to marinate for 10 minutes.
4. In a small bowl, whisk together the remaining 1 tablespoon of rice wine, light soy, peanut butter, garlic, brown sugar, Sichuan peppercorns, ginger, black vinegar, and black beans. Set aside.
5. Heat a wok over medium-high heat until a drop of water sizzles and evaporates on contact.
6. Pour in 2 tablespoons of vegetable oil and swirl to coat the base of the wok. Add the pork and stir-fry for 4 to 6 minutes, until browned and slightly crispy.
7. Pour in the sauce mixture and toss to combine, simmering for 1 minute. Transfer

to a clean bowl and set aside.
8. Wipe out the wok and add 1 tablespoon of vegetable oil. Quickly stir-fry the bok choy for 1 to 2 minutes, until just wilted and tender. Add to the pork bowl and stir together.
9. To assemble, dunk the noodles in the boiling water for 30 seconds to reheat. Drain and divide them among 4 deep bowls. Top each bowl with the pork mixture and drizzle with the chili oil. Top with the chopped peanuts and serve.

Hakka Noodles

Prep Time: 15 Minutes
Cook Time: 15 Minutes
Serves: 4

Ingredients:

- ¾-pound (about 340g) fresh flour-based noodles
- 1 tablespoon peeled finely minced fresh ginger
- ½ red onion, sliced into thin vertical strips
- ½ red bell pepper, sliced into thin strips
- 3 tablespoons sesame oil, divided
- ½ head of green cabbage, shredded
- 1 large carrot, peeled and julienned
- 2 tablespoons light soy sauce
- 1 tablespoon rice vinegar
- 2 teaspoons light brown sugar
- 2 tablespoons vegetable oil
- 2 garlic cloves, finely minced
- 4 scallions, thinly sliced
- 1 teaspoon sriracha
- 1 teaspoon Fried Chili Oil
- Kosher salt
- Ground white pepper

Method:

1. Bring a pot of water to a boil and cook the noodles according to package instructions. Drain, rinse, and toss with 2 tablespoons of sesame oil. Set aside.
2. In a small bowl, stir together the light soy, rice vinegar, brown sugar, sriracha,

chili oil, and a pinch of salt and white pepper. Set aside.
3. Heat a wok over medium-high heat until a drop of water sizzles and evaporates on contact.
4. Pour in the vegetable oil and swirl to coat the base of the wok. Season the oil by adding the ginger and a small pinch of salt. Allow the ginger to sizzle in the oil for about 10 seconds, swirling gently.
5. Add the cabbage, bell pepper, onion, and carrot and stir-fry for 4 to 5 minutes, or until the vegetables are tender and the onion begins to caramelize slightly.
6. Add the garlic and stir-fry until fragrant, about 30 seconds more. Stir in the sauce mixture and bring to a boil.
7. Turn the heat down to medium and simmer the sauce for 1 to 2 minutes. Add the scallions and toss to combine.
8. Add the noodles and toss to combine. Increase the heat to medium-high and stir-fry for 1 to 2 minutes to heat the noodles.
9. Transfer to a platter, drizzle with the remaining 1 tablespoon of sesame oil, and serve hot.

Garlic Noodles

Prep Time: 10 Minutes
Cook Time: 10 Minutes
Serves: 4

Ingredients:

- ½-pound (about 227g) fresh Chinese egg noodles
- ½ teaspoons ground white pepper
- 2 tablespoons sesame oil, divided
- 2 tablespoons light brown sugar
- 2 tablespoons oyster sauce
- 1 tablespoon light soy sauce
- 6 tablespoons unsalted butter
- 8 garlic cloves, finely minced
- 6 scallions, thinly sliced

Method:

1. Bring a pot of water to a boil and cook the noodles according to package directions. Reserve 1 cup of the cooking water, then drain.
2. Drizzle the noodles with 1 tablespoon of sesame oil and toss to coat. Set aside.
3. In a small bowl, stir together the brown sugar, oyster sauce, light soy, and white pepper. Set aside.
4. Heat a wok over medium-high heat and melt the butter until the foaming stops.

5. Add the garlic and half the scallions. Stir-fry for 30 seconds, or until the garlic is softened.
6. Pour in the sauce and stir to combine with the butter and garlic. Bring the sauce to a simmer and add the noodles.
7. Toss the noodles to coat with sauce. If the noodles need to loosen up a bit, add some of the cooking water, 1 tablespoon at a time. Continue to stir-fry the noodles for 2 to 3 minutes, until they are heated through.
8. Transfer the garlic noodles to a platter and garnish with the remaining scallions. Serve hot.

Singapore Noodles

Prep Time: 10 Minutes
Cook Time: 20 Minutes
Serves: 4

Ingredients:

- ½-pound (about 227g) char shiu (Chinese roast pork), sliced into thin strips
- ½-pound (about 227g) medium shrimp, peeled and deveined
- ½-pound (about 227g) dried rice vermicelli noodles
- 1 small white onion, thinly sliced into strips
- ½ green bell pepper, cut into thin strips
- ½ red bell pepper, cut into thin strips
- 1 teaspoon fish sauce (optional)
- 3 tablespoons coconut oil, divided
- 2 garlic cloves, finely minced
- 1 cup frozen peas, thawed
- 2 teaspoons curry powder
- Freshly ground black pepper
- Juice of 1 lime
- 9 fresh cilantro sprigs
- Kosher salt

Method:

1. Bring a large pot of water to boil over high heat. Turn off the heat and add the noodles. Soak for 4 to 5 minutes, until the noodles are opaque.
2. Carefully drain the noodles in a colander. Rinse the noodles with cold water and set aside.
3. In a small bowl, season the shrimp with the fish sauce (if using) and set aside for 5 minutes. If you don't wish to use fish sauce, use a pinch of salt to season the shrimp instead.
4. Heat a wok over medium-high heat until a drop of water sizzles and evaporates

on contact. Pour in 2 tablespoons of coconut oil and swirl to coat the base of the wok. Season the oil by adding a small pinch of salt.
5. Add the shrimp and stir-fry for 3 to 4 minutes, or until the shrimp turn pink. Transfer to a clean bowl and set aside.
6. Add the remaining 1 tablespoon of coconut oil and swirl to coat the wok.
7. Stir-fry the onion, bell peppers, and garlic for 3 to 4 minutes, until the onions and peppers are soft. Add the peas and stir-fry until just heated through, about another minute.
8. Add the pork and return the shrimp to the wok. Toss together with the curry powder and season with salt and pepper. Add the noodles and toss to combine. The noodles will turn a brilliant golden yellow color as you continue to gently toss them with the other ingredients. Continue stir-frying and tossing for about 2 minutes, until the noodles are heated through.
9. Transfer the noodles to a platter, drizzle with the lime juice, and garnish with the cilantro. Serve immediately.

Chinese Birthday Noodles

Prep Time: 10 Minutes
Cook Time: 10 Minutes
Serves: 4

Ingredients:

- 4-ounce (about 115g) char Shiu (Chinese barbecue pork), sliced into thin strips
- 6 to 8 fresh shiitake mushrooms, stems removed and caps thinly sliced
- ½-pound (about 227g) medium shrimp, peeled and deveined
- ½ cup frozen edamame beans, shelled and thawed
- 4 scallions, trimmed, white and green parts thinly sliced
- 3 tablespoons coarsely chopped fresh cilantro
- ¾-pound (about 340g) egg noodles
- 3 tablespoons sesame oil, divided
- 2 tablespoons vegetable oil
- 1 tablespoon light soy sauce
- 2 teaspoons Shaoxing rice wine
- 1 shallot, thinly sliced
- Kosher salt

Method:

1. Bring a pot of water to a boil and cook the noodles according to package

instructions. Drain and rinse the noodles under cold water.
2. Drizzle the noodles with 1 tablespoon of sesame oil and set aside.
3. Heat a wok over medium-high heat until a drop of water sizzles and evaporates on contact. Pour in the vegetable oil and swirl to coat the base of the wok.
4. Add the mushrooms and toss to coat with the oil. Let the mushrooms sit against the wok and sear for 1 to 2 minutes. Toss and flip the mushrooms around for another 30 seconds, or until golden brown.
5. Add the shrimp and shallot and toss with the mushrooms. Stir-fry for 2 to 3 minutes, until the shrimp turns opaque and pink.
6. Season with a pinch of salt. Add the char shui and edamame, tossing and flipping until heated through, about another minute. Drizzle in the light soy and rice wine and toss to coat.
7. Add the scallions and cilantro, reserving a small bit of each for garnish, and toss until the cilantro wilts slightly. Add the noodles and another pinch of salt.
8. Toss and scoop, lifting upward to separate the noodle strands and combine with the shrimp and vegetables.
9. Transfer to a platter and drizzle with the remaining 2 tablespoons of sesame oil. Garnish with the reserved scallions and cilantro. Serve immediately.

Glass Noodles with Napa Cabbage and Green Beans

Prep Time: 15 Minutes
Cook Time: 10 Minutes
Serves: 4

Ingredients:

- ½-pound (about 227g) dried sweet potato noodles or mung bean noodles
- 2 peeled fresh ginger slices, each about the size of a quarter
- 1 small head napa cabbage, chopped into bite-size pieces
- ½-pound (about 227g) green beans, trimmed and halved
- 2 tablespoons light soy sauce
- 2 teaspoons dark soy sauce
- 1 tablespoon oyster sauce
- 2 tablespoons vegetable oil
- 1 teaspoon Sichuan peppercorns
- 3 scallions, coarsely chopped

- 1 teaspoon sugar
- Kosher salt

Method:

1. In a large bowl, soften the noodles by soaking them in hot water for 10 minutes, or until softened.
2. Carefully drain the noodles in a colander. Rinse with cold water and set aside.
3. In a small bowl, mix the light soy, oyster sauce, dark soy, and sugar. Set aside.
4. Heat a wok over medium-high heat until a drop of water sizzles and evaporates on contact. Pour in the oil and swirl to coat the base of the wok.
5. Season the oil by adding the ginger, a small pinch of salt, and the Sichuan peppercorns. Allow the ginger to sizzle in the oil for about 30 seconds, swirling gently. Scoop out the ginger and peppercorns and discard.
6. Add the napa cabbage and green beans to the wok and stir-fry, tossing and flipping for 3 to 4 minutes, until the vegetables are wilted. Pour in the sauce and toss to combine.
7. Add the noodles and toss to combine with the sauce and vegetables. Cover and lower the heat to medium.
8. Cook for 2 to 3 minutes, or until the noodles turn transparent and the green beans are tender.
9. Increase the heat to medium-high and uncover the wok. Stir-fry, tossing and scooping for another 1 to 2 minutes, until the sauce thickens slightly. Transfer to a platter and garnish with the scallions. Serve hot.

Chicken Chow Mein

Prep Time: 15 Minutes
Cook Time: 15 Minutes
Serves: 4

Ingredients:

- ½-pound (about 227g) fresh thin Hong Kong–style egg noodles
- ½-pound (about 227g) chicken thighs, sliced into thin strips
- 1 large handful (3-ounce (about 85g)) mung bean sprouts
- 3 heads of baby bok choy, cut into bite-sized pieces
- 1½ tablespoons sesame oil, divided
- 2 teaspoons Shaoxing rice wine

- 2 teaspoons light soy sauce
- Ground white pepper
- ¼ cup low-sodium chicken broth
- 2 teaspoons dark soy sauce
- 2 teaspoons oyster sauce
- 2 teaspoons cornstarch
- 4 tablespoons vegetable oil, divided
- 2 garlic cloves, finely minced

Method:

1. Bring a pot of water to a boil and cook the noodles according to package instructions. Reserve 1 cup of the cooking water and drain the noodles in a colander.
2. Rinse the noodles with cold water and drizzle in 1 tablespoon of sesame oil. Toss to coat and set aside.
3. In a mixing bowl, combine the rice wine, light soy, and a pinch of white pepper. Toss the chicken pieces to coat and marinate for 10 minutes. In a small bowl, stir together the chicken broth, dark soy, remaining ½ tablespoon of sesame oil, oyster sauce, and cornstarch. Set aside.
4. Heat a wok over medium-high heat until a drop of water sizzles and evaporates on contact. Pour in 3 tablespoons of vegetable oil and swirl to coat the base of the wok. Add the noodles in one layer and fry for 2 to 3 minutes, or until they are golden brown.
5. Flip the noodles over carefully and fry on the other side for 2 more minutes, or until the noodles are crispy and brown, and have formed into a loose cake. Transfer to a paper towel-lined plate and set aside.
6. Add the remaining 1 tablespoon of vegetable oil and stir-fry the chicken and marinade for 2 to 3 minutes, until the chicken is no longer pink and the marinade has evaporated.
7. Add the bok choy and garlic, stir-frying until the bok choy stems are tender, about another minute. Pour in the sauce and toss to combine with the chicken and bok choy.
8. Return the noodles and, using scooping and lifting motion, toss the noodles with the chicken and vegetables for about 2 minutes, until coated with the sauce. If the noodles seem a bit dry, add a tablespoon or so of the reserved cooking water as you toss.
9. Add the bean sprouts and stir-fry, lifting and scooping for 1 more minute. Transfer to a platter and serve hot.

Beef Lo Mein

Prep Time: 15 Minutes
Cook Time: 20 Minutes
Serves: 4

Ingredients:

- ½-pound (about 227g) beef sirloin tips, sliced across the grain into thin strips
- 2 peeled fresh ginger slices, each about the size of a quarter
- ½-pound (about 227g) fresh lo mein egg noodles
- 2 tablespoons sesame oil, divided
- 2 tablespoons Shaoxing rice wine
- 2 tablespoons cornstarch, divided
- 2 tablespoons dark soy sauce
- 3 tablespoons vegetable oil, divided
- ½ red bell pepper, sliced into thin strips
- 1 cup snow peas, strings removed
- 2 garlic cloves, finely minced
- 2 cups mung bean sprouts
- Ground white pepper
- Kosher salt

Method:

1. Bring a pot of water to a boil and cook the noodles according to package instructions. Reserve ½ cup of the cooking water and drain the noodles in a colander.
2. Rinse the noodles under cold water and shake to drain excess water. Drizzle the noodles with 1 tablespoon of sesame oil and toss to coat. Set aside.
3. In a mixing bowl, stir together the rice wine, 2 teaspoons of cornstarch, dark soy, and a generous pinch of white pepper. Add the beef and toss to coat. Set aside for 10 minutes to marinate.
4. Heat a wok over medium-high heat until a drop of water sizzles and evaporates on contact. Pour in the vegetable oil and swirl to coat the base of the wok. Season the oil by adding the ginger and a small pinch of salt. Allow the ginger to sizzle in the oil for about 30 seconds, swirling gently.
5. Add the beef, reserving the marinade, and sear against the wok for 2 to 3 minutes. Toss and flip the beef, stir-frying for 1 more minute, or until no longer pink. Transfer to a bowl and set aside.

6. Add the remaining 1 tablespoon of vegetable oil and stir-fry the bell pepper, tossing and flipping for 2 to 3 minutes, until tender. Add the snow peas and garlic, stir-frying for another minute, or until the garlic is fragrant.
7. Push all of the ingredients to the sides of the wok and pour in the remaining 1 tablespoon of sesame oil, reserved marinade, remaining 4 teaspoons of cornstarch, and ¼ cup of the reserved cooking water. Stir together and bring to a boil.
8. Return the beef to the wok and toss to combine with the vegetables for 1 to 2 minutes, until the sauce becomes thick and glossy.
9. Toss the lo mein noodles with the beef and vegetables until the noodles are coated with the sauce. Add the bean sprouts and toss to combine. Remove and discard the ginger. Transfer to a platter and serve.

Beef Chow Fun

Prep Time: 15 Minutes
Cook Time: 10 Minutes
Serves: 4

Ingredients:

- ¾-pound (about 340g) flank steak or sirloin tips, cut across the grain into ⅛ inch thick slices
- 1½-pound (about 680g) fresh wide rice noodles or ¾-pound (about 340g) dried
- 4 peeled fresh ginger slices, each about the size of a quarter
- 8 scallions, halved lengthwise and cut into 3-inch pieces
- 1½ tablespoons dark soy sauce
- 1½ tablespoons dark soy sauce
- 2 tablespoons sesame oil, divided
- 3 tablespoons vegetable oil, divided
- 2 cups fresh mung bean sprouts
- ¼ cup Shaoxing rice wine
- ¼ cup light soy sauce
- 2 tablespoons cornstarch
- ½ teaspoon sugar
- Ground white pepper
- Kosher salt

Method:

1. In a mixing bowl, stir together the rice wine, cornstarch, dark soy, sugar, light soy, and a pinch of white pepper.
2. Add the beef and toss to coat. Set aside to marinate for at least 10 minutes.
3. Bring a large pot of water to a boil and cook the rice noodles according to package instructions. Reserve 1 cup of the cooking water and drain the rest. Rinse with cold water and drizzle with 1 tablespoon of sesame oil. Set aside.
4. Heat a wok over medium-high heat until a drop of water sizzles and evaporates on contact. Pour in 2 tablespoons of vegetable oil and swirl to coat the base of the wok. Season the oil by adding the ginger and a pinch of salt. Allow the ginger to sizzle in the oil for about 30 seconds, swirling gently.
5. Using tongs, add the beef to the wok and reserve the marinating liquid. Sear the beef against the wok for 2 to 3 minutes, or until a seared, browned crust develops. Toss and flip the beef around the wok for 1 more minute. Transfer to a clean bowl and set aside.
6. Add 1 more tablespoon of vegetable oil and stir-fry the scallions for 30 seconds, or until soft. Add the noodles and lift in a scooping upward motion to help separate the noodles if they have stuck together. Add the cooking water, 1 tablespoon at a time, if the noodles have glued themselves together.
7. Return the beef to the wok and toss to combine with the noodles. Pour in the reserved marinade and toss for 30 seconds to 1 minute, or until the sauce thickens and coats the noodles and they turn a deep, rich brown color. If you need to, add 1 tablespoon of the reserved cooking water to thin out the sauce.
8. Add the bean sprouts and toss until just heated through, about 1 minute. Remove the ginger and discard.
9. Transfer to a platter and drizzle with the remaining 1 tablespoon of sesame oil. Serve hot.

Fried Rice with Egg, Shrimp, and Scallions

Prep Time: 10 Minutes
Cook Time: 10 Minutes
Serves: 4

Ingredients:

- ½-pound (about 227g) shrimp (any size), peeled, deveined, and cut into bite-size pieces
- 1 teaspoon peeled finely minced fresh ginger

- Fried rice is infinitely better with butter!
- 2 tablespoons vegetable oil
- 2 garlic cloves, finely minced
- ½ cup frozen peas and carrots
- 2 scallions, thinly sliced, divided
- 3 cups cold cooked rice
- 3 tablespoons unsalted butter
- 1 tablespoon light soy sauce
- 1 tablespoon sesame oil
- Kosher salt
- 1 large egg, beaten

Method:

1. Heat a wok over medium-high heat until a drop of water sizzles and evaporates on contact.
2. Pour in the vegetable oil and swirl to coat the base of the wok. Season the oil by adding a small pinch of salt. Add the egg and scramble quickly.
3. Push the egg to the sides of the wok to create a center ring and add the shrimp, ginger, and garlic together.
4. Stir-fry the shrimp with a small pinch of salt for 2 to 3 minutes, until they turn opaque and pink. Add the peas and carrots and half the scallions and stir-fry for another minute.
5. Add the rice, breaking up any large lumps, and toss and flip to combine all of the ingredients. Stir-fry for 1 minute, then push it all to the sides of the wok, leaving a well in the bottom of the wok.
6. Add the butter and light soy, let the butter melt and bubble, then toss everything together to coat, for about 30 seconds.
7. Spread the fried rice in an even layer in the wok and let the rice sit against the wok for about 2 minutes to crisp up slightly.
8. Drizzle with the sesame oil and season with another small pinch of salt.
9. Transfer to a platter and serve immediately, garnishing with the rest of the scallions.

Spam Fried Rice

Prep Time: 5 Minutes
Cook Time: 15 Minutes
Serves: 4

Ingredients:

- 2 peeled fresh ginger slices, each about the size of a quarter
- 1 (12-ounce (about 340g)) can Spam, cut into ½-inch cubes

- ½ cup canned pineapple chunks, juices reserved
- ½ white onion, cut into ¼-inch cubes
- 2 garlic cloves, finely minced
- ½ cup frozen peas and carrots
- 2 scallions, thinly sliced, divided
- 3 cups cold cooked rice
- 3 tablespoons unsalted butter
- 2 tablespoons light soy sauce
- 1 teaspoon sriracha
- 1 teaspoon light brown sugar
- 1 tablespoon sesame oil
- 1 tablespoon vegetable oil
- Kosher salt

Method:

1. Heat a wok over medium-high heat until a drop of water sizzles and evaporates on contact. Pour in the vegetable oil and swirl to coat the base of the wok.
2. Season the oil by adding the ginger and a small pinch of salt. Allow the ginger to sizzle in the oil for about 30 seconds, swirling gently.
3. Add the diced Spam and spread it out evenly across the bottom of the wok. Let the Spam sear before tossing and flipping. Continue to stir-fry the Spam for 5 to 6 minutes, until it turns golden and crispy around all sides.
4. Add the onion and garlic and stir-fry for about 2 minutes, until the onion begins to look translucent. Add the peas and carrots and half the scallions. Stir-fry for another minute more.
5. Toss in the rice and pineapple, breaking up any large clumps of rice, and toss and flip to combine all of the ingredients. Stir-fry for 1 minute, then push it all to the sides of the wok, leaving a well in the bottom of the wok.
6. Add the butter, reserved pineapple juice, light soy, sriracha, and brown sugar. Stir to dissolve the sugar and bring the sauce to a boil, then cook for about a minute to reduce the sauce and thicken it slightly. Combine everything to coat, about 30 seconds.
7. Spread the fried rice in an even layer in the wok and let the rice sit against the wok to crisp up slightly, about 2 minutes.
8. Remove the ginger and discard. Drizzle with the sesame oil and season with another small pinch of salt.
9. Transfer to a platter and garnish with the remaining scallions. Serve immediately.

Smoked Trout Fried Rice

Prep Time: 10 Minutes
Cook Time: 10 Minutes
Serves: 4

Ingredients:

- 4-ounce (about 115g) smoked trout, broken into bite-size pieces
- 3 tablespoons ghee or vegetable oil, divided
- 1 teaspoon peeled finely minced fresh ginger
- ½ cup thinly sliced hearts of romaine lettuce
- ½ teaspoon white sesame seeds
- 2 garlic cloves, finely minced
- 3 cups cold cooked rice
- 2 scallions, thinly sliced
- 2 large eggs
- 1 teaspoon sesame oil
- Kosher salt
- Ground white pepper
- 1 tablespoon light soy sauce
- ½ teaspoon sugar

Method:

1. In a large bowl, whisk the eggs with the sesame oil and a pinch each of salt and white pepper until just combined.
2. In a small bowl, stir the light soy and sugar together to dissolve the sugar. Set aside.
3. Heat a wok over medium-high heat until a drop of water sizzles and evaporates on contact. Pour in 1 tablespoon of ghee and swirl to coat the base of the wok.
4. Add the egg mixture and, using a heatproof spatula, swirl and shake the eggs to cook. Transfer the eggs to a plate when just cooked but not dry.
5. Add the remaining 2 tablespoons of ghee to the wok, along with the ginger and garlic. Stir-fry quickly until the garlic and ginger just become aromatic, but take care not to let them burn.
6. Add the rice and soy mixture and stir to combine. Continue stir-frying, for about 3 minutes.
7. Add the trout and cooked egg and stir-fry to break them up, about 20 seconds. Add the lettuce and scallions and stir-fry until they are both bright green.
8. Transfer to a serving platter and sprinkle with the sesame seeds.

Pork Congee

Prep Time: 20 Minutes
Cook Time: 90 Minutes
Serves: 4

Ingredients:

- 1 tablespoon light soy sauce, plus more for serving
- ¾ cup jasmine rice, rinsed and drained
- 2 teaspoons peeled minced fresh ginger
- 6-ounce (about 170g) ground pork
- 2 teaspoons Shaoxing rice wine
- 2 garlic cloves, minced
- 2 teaspoons cornstarch
- 1 teaspoon kosher salt
- 2 tablespoons vegetable oil
- 10 cups water

Optional:

- Pickled Chinese vegetables, thinly sliced, for serving
- Scallion-Ginger Oil, for serving
- Fried Chili Oil, for serving
- Sesame oil, for serving

Method:

1. In a heavy-bottomed pot, bring the water to a boil. Stir in the rice and salt and reduce the heat to a simmer.
2. Cover and cook, stirring occasionally, for about 1½ hours, until the rice has turned to a soft porridge-like consistency.
3. While the congee is cooking, in a medium bowl, stir together the ginger, light soy, rice wine, garlic, and cornstarch.
4. Add the pork and allow it to marinate for 15 minutes.
5. Heat a wok over medium-high heat until a drop of water sizzles and evaporates on contact. Pour in the vegetable oil and swirl to coat the base of the wok.
6. Add the pork and stir-fry, tossing and breaking up the meat, for about 2 minutes.
7. Cook for another 1 to 2 minutes without stirring to get some caramelization.
8. Serve the congee in soup bowls topped with the stir-fried pork. Garnish with your toppings of choice.

Steamed Rice with Bok Choy and Lap Cheung

Prep Time: 2 HOURS
Cook Time: 20 Minutes
Serves: 4

Ingredients:

- 4 lap cheung (Chinese sausage) links or Spanish chorizo
- 4 baby bok choy heads, each sliced into 6 wedges
- 1-inch fresh ginger piece, peeled and finely minced
- 1 garlic clove, peeled and finely minced
- 1 small shallot, thinly sliced
- 2 teaspoons light soy sauce
- 1 tablespoon dark soy sauce
- 2 teaspoons Shaoxing rice wine
- ¼ cup vegetable oil
- 1 teaspoon sesame oil
- 1½ cups jasmine rice
- Sugar

Method:

1. In a mixing bowl, rinse and swish the rice 3 or 4 times under cold water, swishing the rice around in the water to rinse off any starches.
2. Cover the rice with cold water and soak for 2 hours. Drain the rice through a fine-mesh sieve.
3. Rinse two bamboo steamer baskets and their lids under cold water and place one basket in the wok. Pour in 2 inches of water, or enough to make the water level come above the bottom rim of the steamer by ¼ to ½ inch but not so high that the water touches the bottom of the steamer.
4. Line a plate with a piece of cheesecloth and add half the soaked rice to the plate. Arrange 2 sausages and half the bok choy on top, and loosely tie up the cheesecloth so there is enough space around the rice so that it can expand. Place the plate in the steamer basket.
5. Repeat the process with another plate, more cheesecloth, and the remaining sausage and bok choy in the second steamer basket, then stack it on top of the first and cover.
6. Turn the heat to medium-high and bring the water to a boil. Steam the rice for 20 minutes, checking the water level often and adding more as needed.

7. While the rice is steaming, in a small saucepan, heat the vegetable oil over medium heat until it just begins to smoke. Turn off the heat and add the shallot, ginger, and garlic.
8. Stir together and add the light soy, rice wine, sesame oil, dark soy, and a pinch of sugar. Set aside to cool.
9. When the rice is ready, carefully untie the cheesecloth and transfer the rice and bok choy to a platter. Slice the sausages diagonally and arrange on top of the rice. Serve with the ginger soy oil on the side.

Pad See Ew

Prep Time: 20 Minutes
Cook Time: 10 Minutes
Serves: 4

Ingredients:

- ¾-pound (about 340g) flank steak or sirloin tips, sliced across the grain into ⅛-inch-thick slices
- 1 bunch Chinese broccoli (gai lan), stems sliced diagonally into ½-inch pieces, leaves cut
- 1½-pound (about 680g) fresh wide rice noodles or dried rice noodles
- 5 tablespoons vegetable oil, divided
- 2 teaspoons dark soy sauce
- 2 teaspoons cornstarch
- 2 teaspoons fish sauce, divided
- ½ teaspoon kosher salt
- Ground white pepper
- 2 tablespoons oyster sauce
- 1 tablespoon light soy sauce
- ½ teaspoon sugar
- 4 garlic cloves, thinly sliced
- into bite-size pieces
- 2 large eggs, beaten

Method:

1. In a mixing bowl, stir together the dark soy, cornstarch, 1 teaspoon of fish sauce, salt, and a pinch of white pepper.

2. Add the beef slices and toss to coat. Set aside to marinate for 10 minutes.
3. In another bowl, stir together the oyster sauce, light soy, remaining 1 teaspoon of fish sauce, and sugar. Set aside.
4. If using fresh rice noodles, rinse them under hot water to keep them separated, and set aside. If using dried rice noodles, cook them according to package instructions, drain, and set aside.
5. Heat a wok over medium-high heat until a drop of water sizzles and evaporates on contact. Pour in 2 tablespoons of oil and swirl to coat the base of the wok.
6. Using tongs, transfer the beef to the wok and reserve the marinade. Sear the beef against the wok for 2 to 3 minutes, until it's brown and a seared crust develops. Return the beef to the marinade bowl and stir in the oyster sauce mixture.
7. Add 2 more tablespoons of oil and stir-fry the garlic for 30 seconds. Add the Chinese broccoli stems and stir-fry for 45 seconds, keeping everything moving to prevent the garlic from burning.
8. Push the broccoli stems to the sides of the wok, leaving the bottom of the wok empty. Add the remaining 1 tablespoon of oil and scramble the eggs in the well, then toss them together.
9. Add the noodles, sauce, and beef, and toss and flip quickly to combine all of the ingredients, stir-frying for 30 more seconds. Add the broccoli leaves and stir-fry for 30 seconds more, or until the leaves begin to wilt. Return to a platter and serve immediately.

Chapter 2: Soups

Egg Drop Soup

Prep Time: 5 Minutes
Cook Time: 10 Minutes
Serves: 4

Ingredients:

- 2 peeled fresh ginger slices, each about the size of a quarter
- 2 scallions, thinly sliced, for garnish
- 4 cups low-sodium chicken broth
- 2 garlic cloves, peeled
- 2 teaspoons light soy sauce
- 2 tablespoons cornstarch
- 3 tablespoons water
- 2 large eggs, lightly beaten
- 1 teaspoon sesame oil

Method:

1. In a wok or soup pot, combine the broth, garlic, ginger, and light soy and bring to a boil.
2. Reduce to a simmer and cook for 5 minutes. Remove and discard the ginger and garlic.
3. In a small bowl, mix the cornstarch and water and stir the mixture into the wok.
4. Return the heat to medium-high and stir for about 30 seconds, until the soup thickens.
5. Reduce the heat to a simmer. Dip a fork into the beaten eggs and then drag it through the soup, gently stirring as you go.
6. Continue to dip the fork into the egg and drag it through the soup to create the egg threads.
7. When all the eggs have been added, simmer the soup undisturbed for a few moments to set the eggs.
8. Stir in the sesame oil and ladle the soup into serving bowls. Garnish with the scallions.

Sizzling Rice Soup

Prep Time: 20 Minutes
Cook Time: 15 Minutes
Serves: 4

Ingredients:

- 4 fresh shiitake mushrooms, stems removed and caps thinly sliced
- 1 large carrot, peeled and cut into ¼-inch-thick slices
- 2 baby bok choy heads, chopped into bite-size pieces
- 10 to 12 medium shrimp, peeled and deveined
- 4 cups low-sodium chicken broth
- 1 teaspoon Shaoxing rice wine
- 2 teaspoons light soy sauce
- 3 cups vegetable oil
- 2 teaspoons sesame oil
- 1 cup cooked rice

Method:

1. Preheat the oven to 300°F (about 148°C). Line a baking sheet with parchment paper or aluminum foil.
2. Spread the rice in an even layer and bake for 15 to 20 minutes, until it feels dry. Set aside to cool.
3. In a soup pot, bring the chicken broth to a boil over high heat. Lower the heat to medium-high and add the mushrooms and carrots.
4. Add the light soy, sesame oil, and rice wine to the soup and simmer for 5 minutes.
5. Add the bok choy and bring to a boil over high heat. Turn the heat down to simmer and add the shrimp. Stir to distribute the vegetables and shrimp and simmer over low heat while you fry the rice.
6. Pour the oil into the wok; the oil should be about 1 to 1½ inches deep. Bring the oil to 375°F (about 190°C) over medium-high heat. You can tell the oil is at the right temperature by dipping the end of a wooden spoon into the oil. If the oil bubbles and sizzles around it, the oil is ready.
7. Fry the rice a scoopful at a time, until golden brown and crispy, 2 to 3 minutes. Use a wire skimmer to lift the rice in clumps out of the oil and transfer it to a paper towel-lined plate.
8. When ready to serve, divide the soup and vegetables among 4 soup bowls.
9. Top each bowl with the crispy rice and serve while still sizzling.

Beef Noodle Soup

Prep Time: 15 Minutes
Cook Time: 20 Minutes
Serves: 4

Ingredients:

- ¾-pound (about 340g) beef sirloin tips, thinly sliced across the grain
- 4 peeled fresh ginger slices, each about the size of a quarter
- ½-pound (about 227g) dried Chinese noodles (any type)
- 4 tablespoons Shaoxing rice wine, divided
- 4 tablespoons light soy sauce, divided
- 2 teaspoons cornstarch, divided
- Freshly ground black pepper
- 3 tablespoons vegetable oil, divided
- 2 teaspoons Chinese five-spice powder
- 2 garlic cloves, peeled and smashed
- 2 baby bok choy heads, quartered
- 1 tablespoon Scallion-Ginger Oil
- 2 teaspoons baking soda
- 4 cups beef broth
- 1 teaspoon sugar
- Kosher salt

Method:

1. In a small bowl, toss the beef with the baking soda and let it sit for 5 minutes. Rinse the beef and pat dry with paper towels.
2. In another bowl, toss the beef with 1 tablespoon of rice wine, 1 tablespoon of light soy, 1 teaspoon of cornstarch, the sugar, and a pinch each of salt and pepper. Marinate for 10 minutes.
3. In a glass measuring cup, mix the remaining 3 tablespoons of rice wine, 3 tablespoons of light soy, and 1 teaspoon of cornstarch and set aside.
4. Heat a wok over medium-high heat until a drop of water sizzles and evaporates on contact. Pour in 2 tablespoons of vegetable oil and swirl to coat the base of the wok.
5. Add the beef and five spice powder and cook for 3 to 4 minutes, tossing occasionally, until slightly browned. Transfer the beef to a clean bowl and set aside.
6. Wipe the wok clean and return it to medium heat. Add the remaining 1 tablespoon of vegetable oil and swirl to coat the base of the wok. Add the ginger, garlic, and a pinch of salt to season the oil. Allow the ginger and garlic to sizzle in the oil for about 10 seconds, swirling gently.
7. Pour in the soy sauce mixture and bring to a boil. Pour in the broth and return to a boil. Reduce to a simmer and return the beef to the wok. Simmer for 10 minutes.

8. Meanwhile, bring a large pot of water to a boil over high heat. Add the noodles and cook per package instructions. Using a wok skimmer, scoop out the noodles and drain. Add the bok choy to the boiling water and cook for 2 to 3 minutes, until bright green and tender. Scoop out the bok choy and place it in a bowl. Using tongs, toss the noodles with the scallion-ginger oil to coat. Divide the noodles and bok choy into soup bowls.
9. Remove the garlic and ginger from the soup and discard. Divide the meat among the soup bowls, top with the broth, and serve.

Hot-and-Sour Soup

Prep Time: 20 Minutes
Cook Time: 15 Minutes
Serves: 4

Ingredients:

- 4-ounce (about 115g) boneless pork loin, cut into ¼-inch-thick strips
- 4-ounce (about 115g) firm tofu, rinsed and cut into ¼-inch strips
- 1 peeled fresh ginger slice, about the size of a quarter
- 1 tablespoon dark soy sauce
- 4 dried shiitake mushrooms
- 8 dried tree ear mushrooms
- 1½ tablespoons cornstarch
- ¼ cup unseasoned rice vinegar
- 2 tablespoons light soy sauce
- 1 teaspoon Fried Chili Oil
- 1 teaspoon ground white pepper
- 2 tablespoons vegetable oil
- 4 cups low-sodium chicken broth
- 1 large egg, lightly beaten
- 2 scallions, thinly sliced, for garnish
- 2 teaspoons sugar
- Kosher salt

Method:

1. In a bowl, toss the pork and dark soy to coat. Set aside.
2. Place both mushrooms in a heatproof bowl and cover with boiling water. Soak the

mushrooms until softened, about 20 minutes. Pour off ¼ cup of the mushroom water into a glass measuring cup and set aside.

3. Drain and discard the rest of the liquid. Thinly slice the shiitake mushrooms and cut the tree ear mushrooms into bite-size pieces. Return both mushrooms to the soaking bowl and set aside.
4. Stir the cornstarch into the reserved mushroom liquid until the cornstarch has dissolved. Stir in the vinegar, light soy, sugar, chili oil, and white pepper until the sugar has dissolved. Set aside.
5. Heat a wok over medium-high heat until a drop of water sizzles and evaporates on contact. Pour in the vegetable oil and swirl to coat the base of the wok. Season the oil by adding the ginger and a pinch of salt. Allow the ginger to sizzle in the oil for about 30 seconds, swirling gently.
6. Transfer the pork to the wok and stir-fry for about 3 minutes, until the pork is no longer pink. Remove the ginger and discard. Add the broth and bring to a boil. Reduce to a simmer and stir in the mushrooms.
7. Simmer the mushrooms for about 2 minutes. Stir in the tofu and simmer for 2 minutes. Stir in the cornstarch mixture and return the heat to medium-high, stirring until the soup thickens about 30 seconds. Reduce the heat to a simmer.
8. Dip a fork into the beaten egg and then drag it through the soup, gently stirring as you go. Continue to dip the fork into the egg and drag it through the soup to create the egg threads.
9. When all of the egg has been added, simmer the soup undisturbed for a few moments to set the egg threads. Ladle the soup into serving bowls and garnish with the scallions.

Watercress and Pork Soup

Prep Time: 10 Minutes
Cook Time: 4 Hours
Serves: 6 to 8

Ingredients:

- ½-pound (about 227g) pork ribs or pork shoulder, cut into 1-inch pieces
- 1-pound (about 454g) watercress
- 3 pinches ground white pepper
- 12 cups water, divided
- 8 dried red dates

- ¼ cup dried goji berries
- 1 tablespoon salt

Method:

1. in a wok, bring 2 cups of water to a boil.
2. Blanch the pork for about 5 minutes.
3. Rinse the pork and the wok, and set the pork aside.
4. in the wok, bring the remaining 10 cups of water to a boil.
5. Return the pork to the wok.
6. Reduce the heat to low and simmer, partially covered, for 3½ hours.
7. Add the red dates, watercress, goji berries, salt, and pepper.
8. Simmer for 10 more minutes, and serve.

Chinese Mushroom Soup

Prep Time: 10 Minutes
Cook Time: 25 Minutes
Serves: 6 to 8

Ingredients:

- 5 or 6 white or brown button mushrooms, cut into thin slices
- 4 or 5 large shiitake mushrooms, cut into thin slices
- 1 small bunch enoki mushrooms, roots removed
- 8 cups vegetable stock
- ¼ cup dried goji berries
- 2 teaspoons sesame oil
- 1 tablespoon soy sauce
- 1 tablespoon olive oil
- ½ onion, sliced
- 2 garlic cloves, minced
- 1 carrot, cut into thin slices
- 1 teaspoon salt

Method:

1. In a wok over medium heat, heat the olive oil.
2. Sauté the onion and garlic until the onion turns slightly translucent.
3. Add the carrot, shiitake mushrooms, button mushrooms, and enoki mushrooms.

Sauté for about 1 minute.
4. Pour in the vegetable stock and bring to a boil.
5. Add the goji berries, sesame oil, soy sauce, and salt.
6. Simmer over low heat for about 20 minutes before serving.

Lotus Root with Pork Ribs Soup

Prep Time: 10 Minutes
Cook Time: 4 Hours
Serves: 6 to 8

Ingredients:

- 1-pound (about 454g) lotus root, peeled and cut into ¼-inch-thick rounds
- 1-pound (about 454g) pork ribs, cut into 1-inch pieces
- ½ teaspoon peppercorns
- 2 tablespoons soy sauce
- ¼ cup dried goji berries
- 1 teaspoon salt
- 12 cups water
- ½ cup dried red dates (optional)

Method:

1. Place the pork ribs, peppercorns, red dates (if using), lotus root, and water in a wok.
2. Simmer over low heat for at least 4 hours, and up to 6 hours.
3. Turn off the heat and add the soy sauce, salt, and goji berries.
4. Allow the soup to sit for about 15 minutes for the goji berries to reconstitute, then serve.

Sweet Peanut Soup

Prep Time: 5 Minutes, plus 10 to 26 Hours Inactive
Cook Time: 2 Hours
Serves: 4 to 6

Ingredients:

- ½-pound (about 227g) raw peanuts, shelled and skinned
- 8 cups water, plus more for soaking
- 1 tablespoon baking soda
- 4 tablespoons sugar

Method:

1. Soak the peanuts in a bowl of water overnight.
2. Rinse the peanuts, sprinkle them with the baking soda, then cover in fresh water to soak for 1 to 2 more hours.
3. Thoroughly rinse the peanuts.
4. In a wok over high heat, bring the 8 cups of water to a boil.
5. Add the peanuts to the boiling water, reduce the heat to low, and simmer, partially covered, for 2 hours.
6. Add the sugar in increments until the soup reaches your desired sweetness.
7. Serve the soup at room temperature, hot, or cold, with an almond or butter cookie, if desired.

Wonton Soup

Prep Time: 20 Minutes
Cook Time: 10 Minutes
Serves: 6 to 8

Ingredients:

For the Wontons:

- ¼-pound (about 113g) shrimp, peeled, deveined, and roughly chopped
- 20 to 25 square wonton wrappers
- ¼-pound (about 113g) ground pork
- 1 teaspoon cornstarch
- 1 teaspoon sesame oil
- 1 teaspoon soy sauce
- ½ teaspoon salt
- Pinch ground white pepper

For the Soup:

- 8 cups Basic Chinese Chicken Stock, or store-bought
- 2 tablespoons low-sodium soy sauce
- 3 pinches ground white pepper

- 2 teaspoons sesame oil
- 1 scallion, chopped

Method:

To Make the Wontons:

1. in a bowl, mix the pork, cornstarch, sesame oil, shrimp, soy sauce, salt, and pepper.
2. Place about 1 teaspoon of pork mixture in the center of a wonton wrapper.
3. Dampen your finger with water and run it along the edge of the wonton to help seal it, then fold the wonton in half into a triangle. Gently press the edges to seal.
4. Fold the bottom two corners (just outside the meat filling) toward each other, and press those corners together to seal them. Set the wontons aside.

To Make the Soup:

1. Bring the chicken stock to a boil in a wok over high heat. Add the soy sauce and sesame oil.
2. Bring a separate pot of water to a boil. Carefully drop the wontons into the boiling water.
3. As soon as the wontons are cooked, they will float to the top.
4. When they all float to the top, continue boiling for 2 minutes to cook them all the way through.
5. Using a skimmer, carefully transfer the wontons from the water to the chicken stock.
6. Add the pepper and scallion just before serving.

Chicken and Sweet Corn Soup

Prep Time: 10 Minutes
Cook Time: 10 Minutes
Serves: 6 to 8

Ingredients:

- 8 cups Basic Chinese Chicken Stock or store-bought
- 2 (14.75-ounce (about 418g)) cans of cream-style sweet corn
- 2 cups cooked shredded chicken
- 1 teaspoon sesame oil
- 2 eggs, lightly beaten
- 1 scallion, chopped

- 1 teaspoon salt
- 3 teaspoons cornstarch mixed with 2 tablespoons water (optional)

Method:

1. In a wok over high heat, add the corn to the chicken stock and bring to a boil.
2. Add the shredded chicken, salt, and sesame oil. Return to a boil.
3. Stir in the cornstarch mixture (if using) to thicken the soup. Return to a boil.
4. Use chopsticks to stir the soup and while stirring, pour the beaten eggs into the soup. the faster you swirl and the faster you pour, the silkier the egg. Swirl and pour slowly for a chunkier egg texture.
5. Garnish with the chopped scallion just before serving.

Chapter 3: Poultry Recipes

Sesame Oil Chicken

Prep Time: 5 Minutes
Cook Time: 10 Minutes
Serves: 4 to 6

Ingredients:

- 4 chicken drumsticks (bone-in), chopped into 2 or 3 pieces each
- 2-inch piece ginger, peeled and julienned
- 2 tablespoons sesame oil
- 2 tablespoons Shaoxing wine
- 2 teaspoons soy sauce
- ¼ teaspoon dark soy sauce
- Pinch ground white pepper
- ½ cup water

Method:

1. In a wok over medium-high heat, heat the sesame oil.
2. Add the ginger and stir-fry until it turns a very light golden brown.
3. Add the chicken pieces and stir-fry for about 1 minute to cook the surface.
4. Stir in the Shaoxing wine, soy sauce, dark soy sauce, water, and pepper.
5. Stir the chicken well, reduce the heat to low, and simmer until tender, 5 to 10 minutes.
6. Transfer to a serving plate and serve immediately.

Orange Chicken

Prep Time: 5 Minutes, plus 20 Minutes to Marinate
Cook Time: 5 Minutes
Serves: 4 to 6

Ingredients:

For the Marinade:

- 2 (5-ounce (about 142g)) boneless chicken breast halves, cut into bite-size pieces
- 2 pinches ground white pepper
- 3 teaspoons cornstarch
- 2 teaspoons soy sauce

For the Sauce:

- 3 to 4 orange peel strips, julienned
- 2 tablespoons apple cider vinegar
- 1 tablespoon orange juice
- 2 teaspoons brown sugar
- Pinch red pepper flakes
- 2 teaspoons cornstarch
- 1 teaspoon soy sauce
- ½ teaspoon ketchup
- 2 tablespoons water
- 2-star anise petals
- 1 clove

For the Stir-Fry:

- ½ teaspoon toasted sesame seeds
- 2 tablespoons peanut oil
- 1 scallion, chopped

Method:

1. Sprinkle the chicken with the cornstarch, soy sauce, and pepper and toss to combine.
2. Marinate at room temperature for 20 minutes.
3. in a small bowl, make the sauce by mixing the orange peel, water, apple cider vinegar, orange juice, brown sugar, cornstarch, soy sauce, ketchup, star anise, clove, and red pepper flakes. Set it aside.
4. In a wok over medium-high heat, heat the peanut oil.
5. Add the chicken and stir-fry until slightly golden brown. Remove the chicken from the wok and set it aside.
6. Pour the sauce into the wok and stir until it becomes thick.
7. Return the chicken to the wok and stir well to coat each piece.
8. Transfer to a serving plate and garnish with the scallion and sesame seeds.
9. Serve immediately.

Mushroom Chicken

Prep Time: 5 Minutes, plus 20 Minutes to Marinate
Cook Time: 5 Minutes
Serves: 6 to 8

Ingredients:

For the Marinade:

- 2 boneless skinless chicken breast halves, cut into bite-size pieces
- 2 pinches ground white pepper
- 2 teaspoons soy sauce

- 3 teaspoons cornstarch
- ½ teaspoon salt

For the Stir-Fry:

- ½-pound (about 227g) cremini or button mushrooms, cut into quarters or slices
- 1 medium zucchini, cut into bite-size pieces
- 1-inch piece ginger, peeled and minced
- ½ teaspoon toasted sesame seeds
- 2 tablespoons peanut oil
- ½ cup Brown Sauce

Method:

1. Pour the soy sauce, salt, pepper, and cornstarch over the chicken breast and toss to combine.
2. Marinate at room temperature for about 20 minutes.
3. In a wok over medium-high heat, heat the peanut oil.
4. Add the chicken and stir-fry until it turns lightly golden brown on all sides. Remove it from the wok and set it aside.
5. Add the zucchini to the wok and stir-fry until slightly tender, then remove it from the wok and set it aside.
6. Add a little more oil to the wok if needed. Add the ginger and stir-fry for about 20 seconds, then add the mushrooms. Stir-fry the mushrooms until slightly brown.
7. Return the chicken and zucchini to the wok with the mushrooms and stir in the brown sauce.
8. When the sauce thickens, transfer the dish to a serving plate. Top with the sesame seeds.

Black Pepper Chicken with Asparagus

Prep Time: 5 Minutes, plus 20 Minutes to Marinate
Cook Time: 5 Minutes
Serves: 4 to 6

Ingredients:

For the Marinade:

- 2 (5-ounce (about 142g)) boneless skinless chicken breast halves, cut into bite-size pieces
- Pinch freshly ground black pepper

- 3 teaspoons cornstarch
- 2 teaspoons Shaoxing wine
- ½ teaspoon salt

For the Sauce:

- 1 teaspoon freshly ground black pepper
- 1 tablespoon oyster sauce
- 1 teaspoon rice vinegar
- ½ teaspoon soy sauce
- ½ teaspoon dark soy sauce

For the Stir-Fry:

- ½-pound (about 227g) asparagus (about ½ bunch), stems trimmed, cut into 1-inch pieces
- 2 tablespoons peanut oil

Method:

1. Pour the cornstarch, Shaoxing wine, salt, and pepper over the chicken and toss to combine.
2. Marinate at room temperature for 20 minutes.
3. in a small bowl, prepare the sauce by combining the oyster sauce, rice vinegar, soy sauce, dark soy sauce, and pepper, and mix it well. Set it aside.
4. In a wok over medium-high heat, heat the peanut oil.
5. Add the chicken and stir-fry until the chicken is half cooked.
6. Add the asparagus and stir-fry until it turns bright green and the chicken is fully cooked, or for about 2 minutes.
7. Add the sauce to the wok, and stir well to combine all the ingredients.
8. Transfer to a serving dish and serve.

Sweet and Sour Chicken

Prep Time: 5 Minutes, plus 20 Minutes to Marinate
Cook Time: 5 Minutes
Serves: 4 to 6

Ingredients:

- 2 (5-ounce (about 142g)) boneless chicken breast halves, cut into bite-size pieces
- 1 red bell pepper, cut into 1-inch pieces
- ¼ cup Sweet and Sour Sauce

- 1 small onion, cut into wedges
- 2 teaspoons soy sauce
- Pinch ground white pepper
- 2 teaspoons cornstarch
- 2 tablespoons peanut oil
- 2 garlic cloves, minced
- 1 scallion, chopped
- 1 carrot, sliced

Method:

1. Pour the soy sauce, white pepper, and cornstarch over the chicken breast and toss to combine.
2. Marinate at room temperature for about 20 minutes.
3. In a wok over medium-high heat, heat the peanut oil.
4. Add the chicken and stir-fry until slightly golden brown on all sides. Remove it from the wok and set it aside.
5. Add the garlic and stir-fry for about 20 seconds.
6. Add the sweet and sour sauce, followed by the carrot, onion, and bell pepper.
7. Return the chicken to the wok and mix all the ingredients well.
8. Remove from the heat and transfer to a serving plate.
9. Garnish with the chopped scallion.

Chicken with Cashew Nuts

Prep Time: 5 Minutes
Cook Time: 10 Minutes
Serves: 4 to 6

Ingredients:

- 2 boneless skinless chicken breast halves, cut into thin strips
- ½ cup cashews, lightly roasted
- 1½ tablespoons brown sugar
- 2 tablespoons peanut oil
- 2 garlic cloves, minced
- ½ onion, thinly sliced
- 1 tablespoon soy sauce
- 1 tablespoon oyster sauce

- 1 teaspoon fish sauce
- 1 scallion, chopped

Method:

1. In a wok over medium heat, heat the peanut oil.
2. Add the garlic and onion and stir-fry until fragrant.
3. Add the chicken and stir-fry until the chicken is almost fully cooked.
4. Combine the brown sugar, soy sauce, oyster sauce, and fish sauce, and add to the chicken.
5. Increase the heat to high, stir well to mix, and continue stirring until the chicken is fully cooked.
6. Stir in the cashew nuts.
7. Garnish with the chopped scallion, and serve.

Honey Sesame Chicken

Prep Time: 5 Minutes, plus 2 Minutes to Marinate
Cook Time: 5 Minutes
Serves: 4 to 6

Ingredients:

For the Marinade:

- 2 (5-ounce (about 142g)) boneless chicken breast halves
- Pinch ground white pepper
- 3 teaspoons cornstarch
- ½ teaspoon salt
- 1 egg white

For the Sauce:

- 1½ tablespoons apple cider vinegar
- 2 tablespoons honey
- 1 teaspoon soy sauce
- ½ teaspoon sesame oil
- ½ teaspoon salt

For the Stir-Fry:

- 1 teaspoon toasted sesame seeds
- 2 tablespoons peanut oil
- 1 scallion, chopped

Method:

1. Pour the cornstarch, egg white, salt, and pepper over the chicken and toss to combine.
2. Marinate at room temperature for 20 minutes.
3. in a small bowl, prepare the sauce by mixing the honey, apple cider vinegar, sesame oil, soy sauce, and salt.
4. In a wok over medium-high heat, heat the peanut oil.
5. Add the chicken and stir-fry until fully cooked.
6. Stir in the sauce, mixing well to coat the chicken.
7. Sprinkle the sesame seeds over the chicken, stirring well.
8. Transfer to a serving dish and top with the scallion.

Ginger Chicken

Prep Time: 5 Minutes, plus 20 Minutes to Marinate
Cook Time: 5 Minutes
Serves: 4 to 6

Ingredients:

For the Marinade:

- 2 chicken breast halves, cut into bite-size pieces
- 1 teaspoon sesame oil
- Pinch ground white pepper
- 1 tablespoon cornstarch
- ½ teaspoon salt

For the Stir-Fry:

- 2-inch piece ginger, peeled and thinly sliced
- 2 bunches scallions, cut into 1-inch pieces
- 1 tablespoon sesame oil
- 2 tablespoons peanut oil
- 2 tablespoons water
- 1 teaspoon soy sauce

Method:

1. Pour 1 teaspoon of sesame oil, salt, pepper, and cornstarch over the chicken and toss to coat.

2. Marinate at room temperature for about 20 minutes.
3. In a wok over medium-high heat, heat the peanut oil.
4. Add the chicken and stir-fry in two batches until fully cooked.
5. Remove the chicken from the wok and set it aside.
6. Add the remaining 1 tablespoon of sesame oil to the wok.
7. Add the ginger and stir-fry for about 1 minute.
8. Return the chicken to the wok and add the water and soy sauce. Stir-fry until the sauce thickens a little.
9. Add the scallions, stir well to combine, turn off the heat, and serve.

Moo Goo Gai Pan

Prep Time: 5 Minutes, plus 20 Minutes to Marinate
Cook Time: 5 Minutes
Serves: 6 to 8

Ingredients:

For the Marinade:

- 2 boneless chicken breast halves, cut into thin strips
- 2 pinches ground white pepper
- 3 tablespoons cornstarch
- 2 teaspoons soy sauce

For the Sauce:

- ½ cup Basic Chinese Chicken Stock, or store-bought
- 1 teaspoon rice vinegar
- 1 teaspoon Shaoxing wine
- 1 teaspoon cornstarch
- ½ teaspoon salt
- ½ teaspoon sugar

For the Stir-Fry:

- 1-inch piece ginger, peeled and julienned
- 4 to 6 button mushrooms, sliced
- ¼ cup water chestnuts, sliced
- 2 tablespoons peanut oil
- 2 garlic cloves, minced
- 2 cups snow peas
- ¼ cup bamboo shoots

Method:

1. Pour the soy sauce, pepper, and cornstarch over the chicken then toss to coat.
2. Marinate at room temperature for 20 minutes.
3. in a separate bowl, prepare the sauce by mixing the chicken stock, rice vinegar, Shaoxing wine, cornstarch, salt, and sugar. Set it aside.
4. In a wok over medium-high heat, heat the peanut oil.
5. Add the chicken to the wok and stir-fry until almost fully cooked. Remove the chicken from the wok and set it aside.
6. Stir-fry the ginger and garlic for about 15 seconds and add the snow peas.
7. When the snow peas start to turn bright green after about 2 minutes, stir in the mushrooms, bamboo shoots, and water chestnuts.
8. When the mushrooms begin to soften, add the sauce and return the chicken to the wok. Stir-fry to combine all the ingredients.
9. When the sauce has thickened after about 20 seconds, transfer the dish to a serving plate.

General Tso's Chicken

Prep Time: 5 Minutes, plus 20 Minutes to Marinate
Cook Time: 10 Minutes
Serves: 4 to 6

Ingredients:

For the Marinade:

- 2 boneless chicken breast halves, cut into bite-size pieces
- 2 pinches ground white pepper
- 2 teaspoons cornstarch
- ¼ teaspoon salt

For the Sauce:

- 3 teaspoons rice vinegar
- 2 teaspoons hoisin sauce
- 2 teaspoons brown sugar
- 2 teaspoons soy sauce
- 2 tablespoons ketchup

For the Stir-Fry:

- ½ teaspoon toasted sesame seeds

- 2 tablespoons peanut oil
- ¼ dried red chile
- 1 scallion, chopped

Method:

1. in a small bowl, mix the cornstarch, salt, and white pepper.
2. Sprinkle over the chicken, tossing to coat, and marinate at room temperature for 20 minutes.
3. Meanwhile, in a separate small bowl, make the sauce by combining the ketchup, rice vinegar, brown sugar, hoisin sauce, and soy sauce, mixing it well. Set the sauce aside.
4. In a wok over medium-high heat, heat the peanut oil.
5. Add the chicken and stir-fry in batches until fully cooked and slightly brown.
6. Add the chile and pour in the sauce. Stir to coat the chicken in the sauce.
7. Turn off the heat and transfer the dish to a serving plate.
8. Garnish with the sesame seeds and chopped scallion.

Chapter 4: Fish and Seafood

Stir-Fried Fish with Bok Choy and Ginger

Prep Time: 15 Minutes
Cook Time: 15 Minutes
Serves: 4

Ingredients:

- 1-pound (about 454g) boneless fish fillets, cut into 2-inch chunks
- 4 peeled fresh ginger slices, about the size of a quarter
- 3 heads of baby bok choy, cut into bite-size pieces
- 4 tablespoons vegetable oil, divided
- 1 tablespoon Shaoxing rice wine
- 1 large egg white
- 2 teaspoons cornstarch
- 1 teaspoon sesame oil
- ½ teaspoon light soy sauce
- 1 garlic clove, minced
- Kosher salt

Method:

1. In a medium bowl, mix the egg white, cornstarch, sesame oil, rice wine, and light soy.
2. Add the fish to the marinade, and stir to coat. Marinate for 10 minutes.
3. Heat a wok over medium-high heat until a drop of water sizzles and evaporates on contact.
4. Pour in 2 tablespoons of vegetable oil and swirl to coat the base of the wok. Season the oil by adding a small pinch of salt, and swirl gently.
5. With a slotted spoon, lift the fish from the marinade and sear in the wok for about 2 minutes on each side, until lightly browned on both sides. Transfer the fish to a plate and set aside.
6. Add the remaining 2 tablespoons of vegetable oil to the wok. Add another pinch of salt and the ginger and season the oil, swirling gently for 30 seconds.
7. Add the bok choy and garlic and stir-fry for 3 to 4 minutes, tossing constantly, until the bok choy is tender.
8. Return the fish to the wok and gently toss together with the bok choy until combined.
9. Season lightly with another pinch of salt. Transfer to a platter, discard the ginger, and serve immediately.

Whole Steamed Fish with Scallions and Sizzling Ginger

Prep Time: 10 Minutes
Cook Time: 20 Minutes
Serves: 4

Ingredients:

For The Fish:

- 1 whole whitefish, about 2-pound (about 907g), head on and cleaned
- 4 peeled fresh ginger slices, each about the size of a quarter
- ½ cup kosher salt, for cleaning
- 3 scallions, sliced into 3-inch pieces
- 2 tablespoons Shaoxing rice wine

For The Sauce:

- 2 tablespoons light soy sauce
- 1 tablespoon sesame oil
- 2 teaspoons sugar

For The Sizzling Ginger Oil:

- 2 tablespoons peeled fresh ginger finely julienned into thin strips
- 3 tablespoons vegetable oil
- 2 scallions, thinly sliced

Optional:

- Red onion, thinly sliced
- Cilantro

Method:

To Make the Fish:

1. Rub the fish inside and out with the kosher salt. Rinse the fish and pat dry with paper towels.
2. On a plate large enough to fit into a bamboo steamer basket, make a bed using half of each of the scallions and ginger.
3. Lay the fish on top and stuff the remaining scallions and ginger inside the fish. Pour the rice wine over the fish.
5. Rinse a bamboo steamer basket and its lid under cold water and place it in the

wok. Pour in about 2 inches of cold water, or until it comes above the bottom rim of the steamer by about ¼ to ½ inch, but not so high that the water touches the bottom of the basket. Bring the water to a boil.
6. Place the plate in the steamer basket and cover. Steam the fish over medium heat for 15 minutes (add 2 minutes for every half pound more).
7. Before removing from the wok, poke the fish with a fork near the head. If the flesh flakes, it's done. If the flesh still sticks together, steam for 2 minutes more.

To Make the Sauce:

1. While the fish is steaming, in a small pan, warm the light soy, sesame oil, and sugar over low heat, and set aside.
2. Once the fish is cooked, transfer to a clean platter. Discard the cooking liquid and aromatics from the steaming plate.
3. Pour the warm soy sauce mixture over the fish. Tent with foil to keep it warm while you prepare the oil.

To Make the Sizzling Ginger Oil:

1. In a small saucepan, heat the vegetable oil over medium heat. Just before it starts to smoke, add half of each of the ginger and scallions and fry for 10 seconds.
2. Pour the hot sizzling oil over the top of the fish. Garnish with the remaining ginger and scallions and serve immediately.

Pepper and Salt Shrimp

Prep Time: 20 Minutes
Cook Time: 10 Minutes
Serves: 4

Ingredients:

- 1½-pound (about 680g) large shrimp, peeled and deveined, tails left on
- 1 jalapeño pepper, halved and seeded, thinly sliced
- 1½ teaspoons Sichuan peppercorns
- 4 scallions, sliced diagonally
- 6 garlic cloves, thinly sliced
- 1 tablespoon kosher salt
- ½ cup vegetable oil
- 1 cup cornstarch

Method:

1. In a small sauté pan or skillet over medium heat, toast the salt and peppercorns until aromatic, shaking, and stirring frequently to avoid burning. Transfer to a bowl to cool completely.
2. Grind the salt and peppercorns together in a spice grinder or with a mortar and pestle. Transfer to a bowl and set aside.
3. Blot the shrimp dry with a paper towel.
4. In a wok, heat the oil over medium-high heat to 375°F (about 190°C), or until it bubbles and sizzles around the end of a wooden spoon.
5. Put the cornstarch in a large bowl. Just before you are ready to fry the shrimp, toss half the shrimp to coat in the cornstarch and shake off any excess cornstarch.
6. Fry the shrimp for 1 to 2 minutes, until they turn pink. Using a wok skimmer, transfer the fried shrimp to a rack set over a baking sheet to drain. Repeat the process with the remaining shrimp of tossing in cornstarch, frying, and transferring to the rack to drain.
7. Once all of the shrimp have been cooked, carefully remove all but 2 tablespoons of the oil and return the wok to medium heat.
8. Add the scallions, jalapeño, and garlic and stir-fry until the scallions and jalapeño turn bright green and the garlic is aromatic.
9. Return the shrimp to the wok, season to taste with the salt and pepper mixture (you may not use it all), and toss to coat. Transfer the shrimp to a platter and serve hot.

Deep-Fried Oysters with Chili-Garlic Confetti

Prep Time: 15 Minutes
Cook Time: 15 Minutes
Serves: 4

Ingredients:

- 1 (16-ounce (about 453g)) container small shucked oysters
- ½ cup all-purpose flour, divided
- ½ teaspoon baking powder
- Ground white pepper
- ¼ teaspoon onion powder
- ¾ cup sparkling water, chilled

- 1 teaspoon sesame oil
- 3 large garlic cloves, thinly sliced
- 1 small red chili, finely diced
- 1 small green chili, finely diced
- 1 scallion, thinly sliced
- 3 cups vegetable oil
- ½ cup rice flour
- Kosher salt

Method:

1. Drain the shucked oysters in a colander for 10 minutes to remove as much extra liquid as possible.
2. In a mixing bowl, stir together the rice flour, ¼ cup of all-purpose flour, baking powder, a pinch each of salt and white pepper, and onion powder. 3. Add the sparkling water and sesame oil, mix until smooth, and set aside.
4. In a wok, heat the vegetable oil over medium-high heat to 375°F (about 190°C), or until it bubbles and sizzles around the end of a wooden spoon.
5. Blot the oysters with a paper towel and dredge in the remaining ¼ cup of all-purpose flour. Dip the oysters one at a time in the rice flour batter and carefully lower into the hot oil.
6. Fry the oysters for 3 to 4 minutes, or until golden brown. Transfer to a wire cooling rack fitted over a baking sheet to drain. Sprinkle lightly with salt.
7. Return the oil temperature to 375°F (about 190°C) and fry the garlic and chilies briefly until they are crispy but still brightly colored, about 45 seconds. With a wire skimmer, lift out the oil and place it on a paper towel-lined plate.
8. Arrange the oysters on a platter and sprinkle the garlic and chilies over. Garnish with the sliced scallions and serve immediately.

Drunken Shrimp

Prep Time: 30 Minutes
Cook Time: 10 Minutes
Serves: 4

Ingredients:

- 1-pound (about 454g) jumbo shrimp, peeled and deveined, tails left on
- 4 peeled fresh ginger slices, each about the size of a quarter

- 2 tablespoons dried goji berries (optional)
- 2 cups Shaoxing rice wine
- 2 teaspoons sugar
- 2 tablespoons vegetable oil
- Kosher salt
- 2 teaspoons cornstarch

Method:

1. In a wide mixing bowl, stir together the rice wine, ginger, goji berries (if using), and sugar until the sugar is dissolved.
2. Add the shrimp and cover. Marinate in the refrigerator for 20 to 30 minutes.
3. Pour the shrimp and marinade into a colander set over a bowl. Reserve ½ cup of the marinade and discard the rest.
4. Heat a wok over medium-high heat until a drop of water sizzles and evaporates on contact. Pour in the oil and swirl to coat the base of the wok. Season the oil by adding a small pinch of salt, and swirl gently.
5. Add the shrimp and vigorously stir-fry, adding a pinch of salt as you flip and toss the shrimp around in the wok. Keep moving the shrimp around for about 3 minutes, until they just turn pink.
6. Stir the cornstarch into the reserved marinade and pour it over the shrimp. Toss the shrimp and coat with the marinade. It will thicken into a glossy sauce as it begins to boil, about another 5 minutes more.
7. Transfer the shrimp and goji berries to a platter, discard the ginger, and serve hot.

Coconut Curry Crab

Prep Time: 10 Minutes
Cook Time: 15 Minutes
Serves: 4

Ingredients:

- 1 pound (about 454g) canned crabmeat, drained and picked through to remove shell pieces
- 2 peeled slices of fresh ginger, about the size of a quarter
- ¼ cup chopped fresh cilantro or flat-leaf parsley, for garnish
- 1 (13.5-ounce (about 383ml)) can coconut milk

- 1 tablespoon Shaoxing rice wine
- Freshly ground black pepper
- 2 tablespoons vegetable oil
- Kosher salt
- 1 shallot, thinly sliced
- 1 tablespoon curry powder
- ¼ teaspoon sugar
- Cooked rice, for serving

Method:

1. Heat a wok over medium-high heat until a drop of water sizzles and evaporates on contact. Pour in the oil and swirl to coat the base of the wok.
2. Season the oil by adding the ginger slices and a pinch of salt. Allow the ginger to sizzle in the oil for about 30 seconds, swirling gently.
3. Add the shallot and stir-fry for about 10 seconds. Add the curry powder and stir until fragrant for another 10 seconds.
4. Stir in the coconut milk, sugar, and rice wine, cover the wok, and cook for 5 minutes.
5. Stir in the crab, cover with the lid, and cook until heated through, about 5 minutes.
6. Remove the lid, adjust the seasoning with salt and pepper, and discard the ginger.
7. Ladle over the top of a bowl of rice and garnish with chopped cilantro.

Shanghainese-Style Stir-Fried Shrimp

Prep Time: 5 Minutes
Cook Time: 10 Minutes
Serves: 4

Ingredients:

- 1-pound (about 454g) medium-large shrimp, peeled and deveined, tails left on
- 2 tablespoons vegetable oil
- 2 teaspoons Shaoxing rice wine
- 2 scallions, finely julienned
- Kosher salt

Method:

1. Using sharp kitchen scissors or a paring knife, slice the shrimp in half lengthwise, keeping the tail section intact. As the shrimp is stir-fried, cutting it this way will give more surface area and create a unique shape and texture!
2. Blot the shrimp dry with paper towels and keep it dry. The drier the shrimp, the more flavorful the dish. You can keep the shrimp refrigerated, rolled up in a paper towel, for up to 2 hours before cooking.
3. Heat a wok over medium-high heat until a drop of water sizzles and evaporates on contact.
4. Pour in the oil and swirl to coat the base of the wok. Season the oil by adding a small pinch of salt, and swirl gently.
5. Add the shrimp all at once to the hot wok. Toss and flip quickly for 2 to 3 minutes, until the shrimp just begins to turn pink.
6. Season with another small pinch of salt, and add the rice wine. Let the wine boil off while you continue stir-frying, for about another 2 minutes. The shrimp should separate and curl, still attached at the tail.
7. Transfer to a serving platter and garnish with the scallions. Serve hot.

Veggie and Seafood Stir-Fry with Crispy Rice Noodles

Prep Time: 15 Minutes
Cook Time: 15 Minutes
Serves: 4

Ingredients:

- ½-pound (about 227g) shrimp (any size, peeled and deveined) or fish, cut into 1-inch pieces
- ½-pound (about 227g) dried vermicelli rice noodles or bean thread noodles
- 3 peeled fresh ginger slices, each about the size of a quarter
- 1 small white onion, sliced into thin, long vertical strips
- 1 large handful of snow peas, strings removed
- 1 red bell pepper, cut into 1-inch pieces
- 2 large garlic cloves, finely minced
- 1 cup vegetable oil, divided
- Kosher salt
- 1 tablespoon Black Bean Sauce or store-bought black bean sauce (optional)

Method:

1. Heat a wok over medium-high heat until a drop of water sizzles and evaporates on contact. Pour in 2 tablespoons of oil and swirl to coat the base of the wok.
2. Season the oil by adding the ginger slices and a small pinch of salt. Allow the ginger to sizzle in the oil for about 30 seconds, swirling gently.
3. Add the bell pepper and onion and stir-fry quickly by tossing and flipping them around in the wok using a wok spatula. Season lightly with salt and continue to stir-fry for 4 to 6 minutes, until the onion looks soft and translucent.
4. Add the snow peas and garlic, tossing and flipping until the garlic is fragrant, about another minute. Transfer the vegetables to a plate.
5. Heat another 1 tablespoon of oil and add the shrimp or fish. Gently toss and season lightly with a small pinch of salt. Stir-fry for 3 to 4 minutes, or until the shrimp turns pink or the fish begins to flake.
6. Return the vegetables and toss everything together for 1 minute more. Discard the ginger and transfer the shrimp to a platter. Tent with foil to keep warm.
7. Wipe out the wok and return to medium-high heat. Pour in the remaining oil (about ¾ cup) and heat to 375°F (about 190°C), or until it bubbles and sizzles around the end of a wooden spoon.
8. As soon as the oil is at temperature, add the dried noodles. They will immediately begin to puff and rise from the oil. Using tongs, flip the cloud of noodles over if you need to fry the top, carefully lift from the oil, and transfer to a paper towel-lined plate to drain and cool.
9. Gently break the noodles into smaller chunks and scatter over the stir-fried vegetables and shrimp. Serve immediately.

Mussels in Black Bean Sauce

Prep Time: 10 Minutes
Cook Time: 10 Minutes
Serves: 4

Ingredients:

- 2 tablespoons Black Bean Sauce or store-bought black bean sauce
- 2-pound (about 907g) live PEI mussels, scrubbed and debearded
- 2 peeled fresh ginger slices, each about the size of a quarter
- ½ bunch fresh cilantro, coarsely chopped
- 2 scallions, cut into 2-inch-long pieces

- 4 large garlic cloves, thinly sliced
- 2 tablespoons Shaoxing rice wine
- 2 teaspoons sesame oil
- 3 tablespoons vegetable oil
- Kosher salt

Method:

1. Heat a wok over medium-high heat until a drop of water sizzles and evaporates on contact. Pour in the vegetable oil and swirl to coat the base of the wok.
2. Season the oil by adding the ginger slices and a small pinch of salt. Allow the ginger to sizzle in the oil for about 30 seconds, swirling gently.
3. Toss in the scallions and garlic and stir-fry for 10 seconds, or until the scallions are wilted.
4. Add the mussels and toss to coat with the oil. Pour the rice wine down the sides of the wok and toss briefly. Cover and steam for 6 to 8 minutes, until the mussels are opened.
5. Uncover and add the black bean sauce, tossing to coat the mussels. Cover and let steam for another 2 minutes. Uncover and pick through, removing any mussels that have not opened.
6. Drizzle the mussels with the sesame oil. Toss briefly until the sesame oil is fragrant.
7. Discard the ginger, transfer the mussels to a platter, and garnish with the cilantro.

Walnut Shrimp

Prep Time: 15 Minutes
Cook Time: 25 Minutes
Serves: 4

Ingredients:

- 1-pound (about 454g) jumbo shrimp, peeled
- 3 tablespoons sweetened condensed milk
- Nonstick vegetable oil spray
- 25 to 30 walnut halves
- 3 cups vegetable oil, for frying
- 2 tablespoons sugar
- 2 tablespoons water

- ¼ cup mayonnaise
- ¼ teaspoon rice vinegar
- Kosher salt
- ⅓ cup cornstarch

Method:

1. Line a baking sheet with parchment paper and lightly spray with cooking spray. Set aside.
2. Butterfly the shrimp by holding it on a cutting board curved-side down. Starting from the head area, insert the tip of a paring knife three-quarters of the way into the shrimp. Make a slice down the center of the shrimp's back to the tail. Don't cut through the shrimp, and do not cut into the tail area. Open the shrimp like a book and spread it flat. Wipe away the vein (the shrimp's digestive tract) if it is visible and rinse the shrimp under cold water, then blot dry with a paper towel. Set aside.
3. In a wok, heat the oil over medium-high heat to 375°F (about 190°C), or until it bubbles and sizzles around the end of a wooden spoon.
4. Fry the walnuts until golden brown, 3 to 4 minutes, and, using a wok skimmer, transfer the walnuts to a paper towel-lined plate. Set aside and turn off the heat.
5. In a small saucepan, stir together the sugar and water and bring to a boil over medium-high heat, stirring occasionally, until the sugar dissolves.
6. Lower the heat to medium and simmer to reduce the syrup for 5 minutes, or until the syrup is thick and glossy. Add the walnuts and toss to completely coat them with the syrup. Transfer the nuts to the prepared baking sheet and set aside to cool. The sugar should harden around the nuts and form a candied shell.
7. In a small bowl, stir together the mayonnaise, condensed milk, rice vinegar, and a pinch of salt. Set aside.
8. Bring the wok oil back to 375°F (about 190°C) over medium-high heat. As the oil is heating, season the shrimp lightly with a pinch of salt. In a mixing bowl, toss the shrimp with the cornstarch until well coated. Working in small batches, shake the excess cornstarch off the shrimp and fry in the oil, moving them quickly in the oil so they don't stick together. Fry the shrimp for 2 to 3 minutes until golden brown.
9. Transfer to a clean mixing bowl and drizzle the sauce over. Gently fold until the shrimp are evenly coated. Arrange the shrimp on a platter and garnish with the candied walnuts. Serve hot.

Deep-Fried Black Pepper Squid

Prep Time: 10 Minutes
Cook Time: 10 Minutes
Serves: 4

Ingredients:

- 1-pound (about 454g) squid tubes and tentacles, cleaned and tubes cut into ⅓-inch rings
- 2 tablespoons coarsely chopped fresh cilantro
- ¼ teaspoon freshly ground black pepper
- ¾ cup sparkling water, kept ice cold
- ½ cup rice flour
- 3 cups vegetable oil
- Kosher salt

Method:

1. Pour the oil into the wok; the oil should be about 1 to 1½ inches deep. Bring the oil to 375°F (about 190°C) over medium-high heat. You can tell the oil is at the right temperature when the oil bubbles and sizzles around the end of a wooden spoon when it is dipped in. Blot the squid dry with paper towels.
2. Meanwhile, in a shallow bowl, stir the rice flour with a pinch of salt and pepper. Whisk in just enough sparkling water to form a thin batter.
3. Fold in the squid and, working in batches, lift the squid from the batter using a wok skimmer or slotted spoon, shaking off any excess. Carefully lower into the hot oil.
4. Cook the squid for about 3 minutes, until golden brown and crisp. Using a wok skimmer, remove the calamari from the oil transfer it to a paper towel-lined plate, and season lightly with salt. Repeat with the remaining squid.
5. Transfer the squid to a platter and garnish with the cilantro. Serve hot.

Velveted Scallops

Prep Time: 35 Minutes
Cook Time: 5 Minutes
Serves: 4

Ingredients:

- 1-pound (about 454g) fresh sea scallops, rinsed, muscle removed, and patted dry

- 2 scallions, green part only, thinly sliced, for garnish
- 2 tablespoons Shaoxing rice wine, divided
- 3 tablespoons vegetable oil, divided
- 1 tablespoon light soy sauce
- ¼ cup freshly squeezed orange juice
- Grated zest of 1 orange
- 1 large egg white
- 2 tablespoons cornstarch
- 1 teaspoon kosher salt, divided
- Red pepper flakes (optional)

Method:

1. In a large bowl, combine the egg white, 1 tablespoon of rice wine, cornstarch, and ½ teaspoon of salt and stir with a small whisk until the cornstarch completely dissolves and is no longer lumpy.
2. Toss in the scallops and refrigerate for 30 minutes.
3. Remove the scallops from the fridge. Bring a medium-sized pot of water to a boil. Add 1 tablespoon of vegetable oil and reduce to a simmer.
4. Add the scallops to the simmering water and cook for 15 to 20 seconds, stirring continuously until the scallops just turn opaque (the scallops will not be completely cooked through). Using a wok skimmer, transfer the scallops to a paper towel-lined baking sheet and pat dry with paper towels.
5. In a glass measuring cup, combine the remaining 1 tablespoon of rice wine, light soy, orange juice, orange zest, and a pinch of red pepper flakes (if using) and set aside.
6. Heat a wok over medium-high heat until a drop of water sizzles and evaporates on contact. Pour in the remaining 2 tablespoons of oil and swirl to coat the base of the wok. Season the oil by adding the remaining ½ teaspoon salt.
7. Add the velveted scallops to the wok and swirl in the sauce. Stir-fry the scallops until they are just cooked through, about 1 minute.
8. Transfer to a serving dish and garnish with the scallions.

Chapter 5: Pork and Beef Recipes

Five-Spice Pork

Prep Time: 5 Minutes, plus 20 Minutes to Marinate
Cook Time: 5 Minutes
Serves: 4 to 6

Ingredients:

For the Marinade:

- 1-pound (about 454g) pork tenderloin or shoulder, cut into thin strips
- ½ teaspoon Chinese five-spice powder
- Pinch ground white pepper
- 2 teaspoons Shaoxing wine
- 2 teaspoons cornstarch
- ½ teaspoon salt

For the Sauce:

- ½ teaspoon Chinese five-spice powder
- 1 tablespoon soy sauce
- ½ teaspoon brown sugar
- ½ teaspoon dark soy sauce
- 2 teaspoons honey

For the Stir-Fry:

- 2 tablespoons peanut oil
- 2 garlic cloves, minced

Method:

1. Pour the Shaoxing wine, five-spice powder, cornstarch, salt, and pepper over the pork and toss to combine.
2. Marinate at room temperature for 20 minutes.
3. in a small bowl, prepare the sauce by combining the soy sauce, brown sugar, dark soy sauce, honey, and five-spice powder.
4. In a wok over medium-high heat, heat the peanut oil.
5. Add the pork and stir-fry until slightly golden brown.
6. Add the garlic and stir-fry for about 20 seconds.
7. Stir in the sauce, tossing well to coat the pork, and transfer to a serving dish. Serve immediately.

Pork Ribs with Black Bean Sauce

Prep Time: 5 Minutes, plus 20 Minutes to Marinate
Cook Time: 25 Minutes
Serves: 4 to 6

Ingredients:

For the Marinade:

- 2-pound (about 907g) pork ribs, cut into 1½-inch pieces
- 2 teaspoons Shaoxing wine
- Pinch ground white pepper
- 2 teaspoons cornstarch
- ½ teaspoon salt

For the Sauce:

- 2 tablespoons black bean sauce
- 1 teaspoon dark soy sauce
- 2 teaspoons soy sauce
- 2 teaspoons sugar
- 1½ cups water

For the Stir-Fry:

- 1-inch piece ginger, peeled and minced
- 2 tablespoons peanut oil
- 2 garlic cloves, minced
- 1 scallion, chopped

Method:

1. Pour the Shaoxing wine, cornstarch, salt, and pepper over the pork and toss to combine.
2. Marinate at room temperature for about 20 minutes.
3. in a small bowl, prepare the sauce by mixing the water, black bean sauce, sugar, soy sauce, and dark soy sauce. Set it aside.
4. In a wok over medium-high heat, heat the peanut oil.
5. Arrange the pork ribs in the wok in a single layer. Let them cook without stirring for 30 seconds, add the ginger and garlic, then flip the ribs with a wok spatula.
6. Cook, stirring every 10 seconds or so, for about 2 minutes.
7. Add the sauce, stir, and cover the wok.
8. Reduce the heat to low and simmer for about 20 minutes. Peek every few

minutes to make sure the sauce is not evaporating too quickly. If it is, add water when necessary to keep it simmering until the last minute.
9. Transfer the ribs to a serving plate and garnish with the chopped scallion. Serve immediately.

Steamed Egg with Ground Pork

Prep Time: 5 Minutes, plus 15 Minutes to Marinate
Cook Time: 15 Minutes
Serves: 4 to 6

Ingredients:

- Pinch freshly ground black pepper
- 1 teaspoon Shaoxing wine
- ½-pound (about 227g) ground pork
- 2 teaspoons soy sauce
- 1 teaspoon cornstarch
- ½ teaspoon salt
- 3 eggs
- ½ cup water
- 2 teaspoons finely diced Chinese preserved radish (optional)

Method:

1. in a medium bowl, combine the ground pork, preserved radish (if using), cornstarch, soy sauce, salt, and pepper, mixing it well.
2. Marinate at room temperature for about 15 minutes.
3. Set up a steaming rack in a wok, fill it with water halfway up to the rack, and set the heat to medium.
4. in a separate bowl, whisk the eggs with the water and Shaoxing wine. Set it aside.
5. Transfer the ground pork mixture to a shallow heatproof dish. Spread the ground pork in a single layer to cover the dish.
6. Pour the egg mixture evenly over the ground pork.
7. Cover the dish with aluminum foil. This will prevent water from dripping onto the custard.
8. When the water in the wok starts to boil, place the dish on the steaming rack.
9. Steam for about 15 minutes or until the custard is set, then serve.

Sichuan Twice-Cooked Pork

Prep Time: 25 Minutes
Cook Time: 5 Minutes
Serves: 4

Ingredients:

- 1-pound (about 454g) pork shoulder
- Water for boiling pork shoulder

For the Sauce:

- 1 tablespoon black bean paste
- 1 teaspoon chili bean paste
- 1 tablespoon soy sauce
- ½ teaspoon sugar
- Pinch salt

For the Stir-Fry:

- 1 green bell pepper, cut into bite-size pieces
- 1 leek, cut into 1-inch pieces
- 1 tablespoon peanut oil
- 2 garlic cloves, minced

Method:

1. Fill a medium pot with enough water to cover the pork shoulder.
2. Bring the water to a boil over high heat and lower the pork into the pot. Reduce the heat to medium, cover, and simmer for 20 minutes.
3. Remove the pork from the water and let it cool. Keep it in the refrigerator until you are ready to cook the dish.
4. in a small bowl, prepare the sauce by mixing the black bean paste, chili bean paste, soy sauce, sugar, and salt.
5. When the meat has cooled and you are ready to prepare the dish, slice it into the thinnest pieces possible with a very sharp knife.
6. In a wok over medium-high heat, heat the peanut oil. Add the pork and stir-fry the slices until they turn slightly brown around the edges. Remove the pork from the wok and set it aside.
7. Add more oil to the wok if needed, add the garlic, and stir-fry for about 20 seconds, until aromatic.
8. Add the leek and bell pepper, stir-fry for about 1 minute, and return the pork to the wok.
9. Add the black bean sauce, stir well, and transfer the dish to a serving plate.

Peking-Style Pork Ribs

Prep Time: 5 Minutes, plus 20 Minutes to Marinate
Cook Time: 5 Minutes
Serves: 4 to 6

Ingredients:

For the Marinade:

- 2-pound (about 907g) pork ribs, cut into about 1½-inch pieces
- 2 teaspoons Chinese rose wine
- Pinch ground white pepper
- ¼ teaspoon five-spice powder
- 3 teaspoons cornstarch
- ½ teaspoon salt

For the Sauce:

- 1½ tablespoons apple cider vinegar
- 2 teaspoons brown sugar
- ½ teaspoon dark soy sauce
- 1 teaspoon soy sauce
- 2 tablespoons ketchup
- Pinch five-spice powder

For the Stir-Fry:

- 2 tablespoons peanut oil
- 2 garlic cloves, minced

Method:

1. Pour the Chinese rose wine over the pork. Add the salt, pepper, and five-spice powder.
2. Mix well, then coat the pork with the cornstarch. Marinate at room temperature for 20 minutes.
3. in a small bowl, prepare the sauce by mixing the ketchup, apple cider vinegar, soy sauce, dark soy sauce, brown sugar, and five-spice powder.
4. In a wok over medium-high heat, heat the peanut oil.
5. Arrange the pork ribs in the wok in a single layer.
6. Cook without stirring for about 30 seconds, reduce the heat to medium, and stir-fry for about 5 minutes or until the pork is cooked and golden brown.
7. Add the garlic and stir-fry for about 20 seconds until aromatic.
8. Stir in the sauce, coating the ribs.
9. Transfer the ribs and sauce to a serving plate.

Pork and Mixed Vegetable Stir-Fry

Prep Time: 5 Minutes, plus 20 Minutes to Marinate
Cook Time: 5 Minutes
Serves: 4 to 6

Ingredients:

For the Marinade:

- ½-pound (about 227g) boneless pork chop, cut into thin strips
- Pinch ground white pepper
- 2 teaspoons cornstarch
- ½ teaspoon salt

For the Stir-Fry:

- 2 to 3 tablespoons All Purpose Stir-Fry Sauce
- 1-inch piece ginger, peeled and julienned
- 1 small head of broccoli, cut into florets
- ½ teaspoon toasted sesame seeds
- 1 small onion, cut into wedges
- 2 garlic cloves, minced
- 2 tablespoons peanut oil
- 1 tablespoon water
- 1 red bell pepper, sliced
- 1 cup snow peas

Method:

1. Sprinkle the cornstarch, salt, and pepper evenly over the pork and mix to combine. Marinate at room temperature for 20 minutes.
2. In a wok over medium-high heat, heat the peanut oil.
3. Add the pork and stir-fry until fully cooked. Remove the pork from the wok and set it aside.
4. Add the ginger and garlic to the wok and stir-fry for about 20 seconds, until aromatic.
5. Add the broccoli florets, stir-fry for a few seconds, and add the water to help steam the broccoli.
6. Add the bell pepper, snow peas, and onion, and stir-fry until the onion turns slightly translucent.
7. Return the pork to the wok and add the stir-fry sauce.
8. Toss for a few seconds to combine all the ingredients, then transfer the dish to a serving plate.
9. Sprinkle the sesame seeds on top just before serving.

Moo Shu Pork Lettuce Wraps

Prep Time: 5 Minutes, plus 20 Minutes to Marinate
Cook Time: 5 Minutes
Serves: 4 to 6

Ingredients:

- 1 head lettuce

For the Marinade:

- 1 pound (about 454g) pork tenderloin, cut into thin strips (like French fries)
- 2 teaspoons Shaoxing wine
- 2 teaspoons cornstarch
- 2 teaspoons soy sauce
- Pinch ground white pepper
- ½ teaspoon salt

For the Sauce:

- 2 tablespoons hoisin sauce
- 1 tablespoon rice vinegar
- 1 tablespoon oyster sauce
- 1 teaspoon soy sauce
- ½ teaspoon sesame oil
- 1 teaspoon sugar

For the Stir-Fry:

- 4 or 5 large shiitake mushrooms, thinly sliced
- 2-inch piece ginger, peeled and julienned
- ½ cup chopped fresh cilantro
- 2 tablespoons peanut oil
- 2 garlic cloves, minced
- 4 cups shredded cabbage
- ½ carrot, julienned
- 1 scallion, chopped

Method:

1. Separate and wash the lettuce leaves. Chill the leaves in the refrigerator until ready to serve.
2. Pour the soy sauce, Shaoxing wine, cornstarch, salt, and pepper over the pork and toss to combine and coat the meat. Marinate at room temperature for 20

minutes.
3. Meanwhile, in a small bowl, make the sauce by mixing the hoisin sauce, rice vinegar, sugar, soy sauce, oyster sauce, and sesame oil. Set it aside.
4. In a wok over medium-high heat, heat the peanut oil.
5. Add the ginger and garlic and stir-fry until aromatic, or for about 20 seconds.
6. Add the pork and stir-fry for about 30 seconds. Toss in the sliced shiitake mushrooms.
7. Once the pork and mushrooms are cooked all the way through, stir in the sauce and mix well.
8. Toss in the shredded cabbage and carrot, stir, and turn off the heat.
9. Transfer to a serving dish, garnish with the chopped scallion and cilantro, and serve with the chilled lettuce.

Sweet and Sour Pork

Prep Time: 5 Minutes, plus 20 Minutes to Marinate
Cook Time: 10 Minutes
Serves: 4 to 6

Ingredients:

For the Marinade:

- 1 pound (about 454g) pork tenderloin or pork shoulder, cut into ¾-inch pieces
- Pinch ground white pepper
- 2 teaspoons Shaoxing wine
- 2 teaspoons cornstarch
- ½ teaspoon salt

For the Stir-Fry:

- 1 (8-ounce (about 225g)) can pineapple chunks, drained
- 1 green or yellow bell pepper, cut into 1-inch pieces
- 1 small onion, cut into wedges
- ¼ cup Sweet and Sour Sauce
- 1 scallion, cut into 1-inch pieces
- 2 tablespoons peanut oil
- 2 garlic cloves, minced

Method:

1. Pour the Shaoxing wine, cornstarch, salt, and pepper over the pork and toss to

combine.
2. Marinate at room temperature for about 20 minutes.
3. In a wok over medium-high heat, heat the peanut oil.
4. Add the pork in batches to the wok in a single layer. Allow the bottom of the pork to cook through before flipping. Stir-fry until fully cooked, then remove the pork from the wok and set it aside.
5. Stir-fry the garlic for about 20 seconds until aromatic, adding a touch more oil if necessary.
6. Add the pineapple chunks, onion, and bell pepper to the wok. Stir-fry until the onions are slightly translucent.
7. Stir in the sweet and sour sauce, mixing well to combine.
8. Return the cooked pork to the wok along with the scallion. Stir to combine all the ingredients.
9. Transfer to a serving dish and serve immediately.

Beef with Broccoli

Prep Time: 5 Minutes, plus 20 Minutes to Marinate
Cook Time: 5 Minutes
Serves: 6

Ingredients:

For the Marinade:

- ½-pound (about 227g) tenderloin or sirloin steak, thinly sliced
- Pinch freshly ground black pepper
- 2 teaspoons cornstarch
- 1 teaspoon soy sauce

For the Stir-Fry:

- 2 heads broccoli, cut into florets
- 1½ tablespoons peanut oil
- 3 garlic cloves, minced
- ½ cup Brown Sauce
- ¼ cup water

Method:

1. Pour the cornstarch, soy sauce, and pepper over the beef and toss to combine.
2. Marinate at room temperature for 20 minutes.

3. In a wok over medium-high heat, heat the peanut oil.
4. Add the beef and stir-fry just until no longer pink. Remove the beef from the wok and set it aside.
5. Add the garlic and stir-fry for 2 or 3 seconds.
6. Add the broccoli florets and water to help steam the broccoli.
7. When the water has evaporated, return the beef to the wok.
8. Add the brown sauce and give everything a good stir.
9. As soon as the sauce thickens, turn off the heat and transfer the dish to a serving plate.

Mongolian Beef

Prep Time: 5 Minutes, plus 20 Minutes to Marinate
Cook Time: 5 Minutes
Serves: 4

Ingredients:

For the Marinade:

- 1-pound (about 454g) flank steak or sirloin steak, thinly sliced
- Pinch freshly ground black pepper
- 2 teaspoons cornstarch
- ½ teaspoon salt

For the Sauce:

- 1 tablespoon soy sauce
- 1 teaspoon brown sugar
- 1 teaspoon rice vinegar
- 1 tablespoon water

For the Stir-Fry:

- 1-inch piece ginger, peeled and julienned
- 1 scallion, cut into 1-inch pieces
- 2 garlic cloves, minced
- 2 tablespoons peanut oil

Method:

1. Sprinkle the cornstarch, salt, and pepper over the beef and toss to combine.
2. Marinate at room temperature for 20 minutes.
3. in a small bowl, prepare the sauce by mixing the soy sauce, water, brown sugar,

and rice vinegar.
4. In a wok over medium-high heat, heat the peanut oil.
5. Add the beef and fry just until the surfaces turn brown.
6. Add the ginger and garlic, and stir-fry until fragrant, 2 or 3 seconds.
7. Add the sauce and stir to coat the beef.
8. Turn off the heat and add the scallion. Give it one last stir to very lightly heat up the scallions but not to cook them.
9. Transfer the dish to a serving plate.

Beef with Shiitake Mushrooms

Prep Time: 5 Minutes, plus 20 Minutes to Marinate
Cook Time: 5 Minutes
Serves: 4 to 6

Ingredients:

- 2 cups whole dried shiitake mushrooms
- 5 cups boiling water

For the Marinade:

- 1-pound (about 454g) beef tenderloin or sirloin, cut into thin strips
- Pinch freshly ground black pepper
- 2 teaspoons soy sauce
- 2 teaspoons cornstarch

For the Sauce:

- 2 tablespoons oyster sauce
- 1 tablespoon soy sauce
- 2 teaspoons brown sugar
- ½ teaspoon sesame oil

For the Stir-Fry:

- 2 tablespoons peanut oil
- 1 scallion, chopped

Method:

1. Soak the dried shiitake mushrooms in boiling water for about 20 minutes.
2. Meanwhile, pour the soy sauce, cornstarch, and pepper over the beef, and toss to combine. Marinate at room temperature for about 20 minutes.
3. in a small bowl, make the sauce by mixing the oyster sauce, soy sauce, brown

sugar, and sesame oil. Set it aside.
4. Drain and discard the water from the mushrooms, cut off and discard the mushroom stems, and gently squeeze the caps to remove excess water. Cut the mushrooms into thin slices.
5. In a wok over medium-high heat, heat the peanut oil.
6. Add the beef and stir-fry for about 30 seconds, then remove it from the wok.
7. Add the sliced mushrooms, along with a little more peanut oil if needed. Stir-fry for about 2 minutes, then stir in the sauce.
8. Return the beef to the wok, toss to combine all the ingredients, and transfer to a serving dish.
9. Garnish with the chopped scallion and serve immediately.

Beef and Bell Pepper Stir-Fry

Prep Time: 5 Minutes, plus 20 Minutes to Marinate
Cook Time: 5 Minutes
Serves: 4 to 6

Ingredients:

For the Marinade:

- 1-pound (about 454g) flank steak, thinly sliced
- ½ teaspoon ground black pepper
- 2 teaspoons cornstarch
- ½ teaspoon salt

For the Stir-Fry:

- 1 red bell pepper, cut into thin strips
- 1 green bell pepper, cut into thin strips
- 1 onion, cut into rings
- 2 tablespoons peanut oil
- 2 cloves garlic, minced
- 1 fresh red or green chile, cut into strips (optional)

For the Sauce:

- 1 teaspoon black bean sauce
- ½ teaspoon dark soy sauce
- 1 tablespoon soy sauce
- ½ teaspoon sugar
- ½ teaspoon sesame oil

Method:

1. Sprinkle the cornstarch, salt, and pepper over the beef, and toss to combine.
2. Marinate at room temperature for about 20 minutes.
3. in a small bowl, prepare the sauce by mixing the soy sauce, black bean sauce, sugar, dark soy sauce, and sesame oil. Set it aside.
4. In a wok over high heat, heat the peanut oil.
5. Arrange the beef in the wok in a single layer.
6. Cook without stirring for about 20 seconds, flip the beef, and continue to stir-fry until fully cooked, about 1 minute.
7. Remove the beef from the wok.
8. Add a little more oil to the wok if needed, then add the garlic, red and green bell peppers, chile (if using), and onion. Avoid stirring too much, just toss lightly so the high heat can blister the peppers.
9. Return the beef to the wok and add the sauce. Stir to combine all the ingredients and transfer to a serving dish.

Sichuan Beef

Prep Time: 5 Minutes, plus 15 Minutes to Marinate
Cook Time: 5 Minutes
Serves: 4

Ingredients:

For the Marinade:

- 1-pound (about 454g) beef tenderloin or sirloin, cut into ¼-inch strips (like French fries)
- 2 teaspoons cornstarch
- 1 teaspoon sesame oil
- 1 teaspoon soy sauce

For the Sauce:

- ½ tablespoon oyster sauce
- ¼ teaspoon dark soy sauce
- 1 tablespoon soy sauce
- 1 teaspoon brown sugar
- 1 teaspoon sesame oil
- 1 teaspoon chili oil

For the Stir-Fry:

- 2 tablespoons peanut oil
- 2 garlic cloves, minced
- 5 or 6 dried red chiles
- ½ carrot, julienned
- 1 scallion, chopped

Method:

1. Pour the cornstarch, sesame oil, and soy sauce over the beef and toss to combine.
2. Marinate at room temperature for 15 minutes.
3. in a small bowl, prepare the sauce by mixing the soy sauce, brown sugar, sesame oil, chili oil, oyster sauce, and dark soy sauce. Set it aside.
4. In a wok over medium-high heat, heat the peanut oil.
5. Add the beef and stir-fry for about 30 seconds.
6. Add the garlic and stir-fry until the beef is almost cooked.
7. Add the sauce and dried red chiles, tossing to combine all the ingredients.
8. Turn off the heat, add the carrot, and give the dish one last stir.
9. Transfer the beef to a serving plate and garnish with the chopped scallion.

Beef with Honey and Black Pepper Sauce

Prep Time: 5 Minutes, plus 15 Minutes to Marinate
Cook Time: 5 Minutes
Serves: 4 to 6

Ingredients:

For the Marinade:

- 1-pound (about 454g) of beef tenderloin or steak, cut into thin slices
- 3 teaspoons cornstarch
- ¼ teaspoon black pepper
- ½ teaspoon salt

For the Sauce:

- 2½ tablespoons low-sodium soy sauce
- 1 teaspoon freshly ground black pepper
- 2 tablespoons water
- 2 teaspoons oyster sauce

- 3 tablespoons honey

For the Stir-Fry:

- 2 tablespoons peanut oil
- ½ onion, thinly sliced
- 2 garlic cloves, minced

Method:

1. Sprinkle the cornstarch, salt, and pepper over the beef and toss to combine.
2. Marinate at room temperature for 15 minutes.
3. in a small bowl, prepare the sauce by mixing the honey, soy sauce, water, oyster sauce, and pepper.
4. In a wok over medium-high heat, heat the peanut oil.
5. Add the beef and stir-fry until just browned, remove from the wok, and set it aside.
6. Toss the onion and garlic into the wok and stir-fry until the onion turns slightly translucent.
7. Return the beef to the wok and add the sauce, stirring to coat the beef.
8. Turn off the heat and transfer to a serving plate.

Chapter 6: Tofu and Vegetables

Ma Po Tofu

Prep Time: 10 Minutes
Cook Time: 20 Minutes
Serves: 4

Ingredients:

- 1 pound (about 454g) medium tofu, drained and cut into ½-inch cubes
- 3 tablespoons doubanjiang (Chinese chili bean paste)
- 1 teaspoon peeled finely minced fresh ginger
- 1 tablespoon Sichuan peppercorns, crushed
- ½-pound (about 227g) ground pork
- 2 tablespoons Shaoxing rice wine
- ½ teaspoon Chinese five-spice powder
- 1½ cups low-sodium chicken broth
- 2 teaspoons light soy sauce
- 2 teaspoons cornstarch
- 1½ tablespoons water
- 2 tablespoons vegetable oil
- 4 scallions, thinly sliced, divided
- 1 teaspoon chili oil
- 1 teaspoon sugar
- Kosher salt
- 1 tablespoon coarsely chopped fresh cilantro leaves, for garnish

Method:

1. In a small bowl, mix the ground pork, rice wine, light soy, and ginger. Set aside.
2. In another small bowl, mix the cornstarch with the water. Set aside.
3. Heat a wok over medium-high heat and pour in the vegetable oil. Add the Sichuan peppercorns and sauté gently until they begin to sizzle as the oil heats up.
4. Add the marinated pork and bean paste and stir-fry for 4 to 5 minutes, until the pork is browned and crumbled.
5. Add half the scallions, the chili oil, sugar, and five spice powder. Continue to stir-fry for another 30 seconds, or until the scallions wilt.
6. Scatter the tofu cubes over the pork and pour in the broth. Do not stir; let the tofu cook and firm up a bit first.
7. Cover and simmer for 15 minutes over medium heat. Uncover and stir gently. Be

careful not to break up the tofu cubes too much.
8. Taste and add salt or sugar, depending on your preference. Additional sugar can calm down the spiciness if it's too hot. Stir the cornstarch and water again and add to the tofu. Gently stir until the sauce thickens.
9. Garnish with the remaining scallions and cilantro and serve hot.

Tofu and Eggplant in Sizzling Garlic Sauce

Prep Time: 15 Minutes
Cook Time: 15 Minutes
Serves: 4

Ingredients:

- 3 long Chinese eggplants (about ¾-pound (about 340g)), trimmed and sliced diagonally into 1-inch pieces
- ½-pound (about 227g) firm tofu, cut into ½-inch cubes
- 1 teaspoon peeled minced fresh ginger
- 3 tablespoons vegetable oil, divided
- 1½ tablespoons cornstarch, divided
- 6 cups water plus 1 tablespoon, divided
- 1 tablespoon kosher salt
- 1 tablespoon light soy sauce
- 2 teaspoons sugar
- ½ teaspoon dark soy sauce
- 3 garlic cloves, chopped

Method:

1. In a large bowl, combine the 6 cups of water and salt. Stir briefly to dissolve the salt and add the eggplant pieces.
2. Place a large pot lid on top to keep the eggplant submerged in the water and let sit for 15 minutes.
3. Drain the eggplant and pat dry with paper towels. Toss the eggplant in a bowl with a dusting of cornstarch, about 1 tablespoon.
4. In a small bowl, stir the remaining ½ tablespoon cornstarch with the remaining 1 tablespoon of water, light soy, sugar, and dark soy. Set aside.
5. Heat a wok over medium-high heat until a drop of water sizzles and evaporates on contact. Pour in 2 tablespoons of oil and swirl to coat the base of the wok and

up its sides. Arrange the eggplant in a single layer in the wok.
6. Sear the eggplant on each side, about 4 minutes per side. The eggplant should be slightly charred and golden brown. Lower the heat to medium if the wok begins to smoke. Transfer the eggplant to a bowl and return the wok to the heat.
7. Add the remaining 1 tablespoon of oil and stir-fry the garlic and ginger until they are fragrant and sizzling about 10 seconds. Add the tofu and stir-fry for 2 minutes more, then return the eggplant to the wok.
8. Stir the sauce again and pour into the wok, tossing all the ingredients together until the sauce thickens to a dark, glossy consistency.
9. Transfer the eggplant and tofu to a platter and serve hot.

Hunan-Style Tofu

Prep Time: 15 Minutes
Cook Time: 10 Minutes
Serves: 4

Ingredients:

- 1 pound (about 454g) of firm tofu, drained and cut into ½-inch-thick squares, 2 inches across
- 3 tablespoons fermented black beans, rinsed and smashed
- 2 tablespoons doubanjiang (Chinese chili bean paste)
- 1-inch piece of fresh ginger, peeled and finely minced
- 4 tablespoons vegetable or canola oil, divided
- 1 large red bell pepper, cut into 1-inch pieces
- ¼ cup low-sodium chicken or vegetable broth
- 4 scallions, cut into 2-inch sections
- 1 tablespoon Shaoxing rice wine
- 3 garlic cloves, finely minced
- 1 teaspoon sugar
- 1 teaspoon cornstarch
- 1 tablespoon water
- Kosher salt

Method:

1. In a small bowl, stir together the cornstarch and water and set aside.
2. Heat a wok over medium-high heat until a drop of water sizzles and evaporates on contact. Pour in 2 tablespoons of oil and swirl to coat the base and sides of the wok.
3. Add a pinch of salt and arrange the tofu slices in the wok in one layer. Sear the

tofu for 1 to 2 minutes, tilting the wok around to slip the oil under the tofu as it sears.
4. When the first side is browned, using a wok spatula, carefully flip the tofu and sear for another 1 to 2 minutes until golden brown. Transfer the seared tofu to a plate and set aside.
5. Lower the heat to medium-low. Add the remaining 2 tablespoons of oil to the wok. As soon as the oil begins to slightly smoke, add the black beans, bean paste, ginger, and garlic. Stir-fry for 20 seconds, or until the oil takes on a deep red color from the bean paste.
6. Add the bell pepper and scallions and toss with the Shaoxing wine and sugar. Cook for another minute, or until the wine is nearly evaporated and the bell pepper is tender.
7. Gently fold in the fried tofu until all the ingredients in the wok are combined. Continue to cook for 45 seconds more, or until the tofu takes on a deep red color and the scallions have wilted.
8. Drizzle the chicken broth over the tofu mixture and gently stir to deglaze the wok and dissolve any of the stuck bits on the wok. Give the cornstarch-water mixture a quick stir and add to the wok.
9. Gently stir and simmer for 2 minutes, or until the sauce becomes glossy and thick. Serve hot.

Steamed Bean Curd in a Simple Sauce

Prep Time: 10 Minutes
Cook Time: 10 Minutes
Serves: 4

Ingredients:

- 1 tablespoon coarsely chopped fresh cilantro leaves
- 1 teaspoon peeled finely minced fresh ginger
- 1-pound (about 454g) medium tofu
- 2 tablespoons light soy sauce
- 1 tablespoon sesame oil
- 2 teaspoons black vinegar
- 2 garlic cloves, finely minced
- ½ teaspoon sugar
- 2 scallions, thinly sliced

Method:

1. Remove the tofu from its packaging, taking care to keep it intact. Place it on a large plate and carefully slice it into 1- to 1½-inch-thick slices.
2. Set aside for 5 minutes. Resting the tofu allows more of its whey to drain out.
3. Rinse a bamboo steamer basket and its lid under cold water and place it in the wok. Pour in about 2 inches of cold water, or until it comes above the bottom rim of the steamer by about ¼ to ½ inch, but not so high that the water touches the bottom of the basket.
4. Drain any extra whey from the tofu plate and place the plate in the bamboo steamer.
5. Cover and set the wok over medium-high heat. Bring the water to a boil and steam the tofu for 6 to 8 minutes.
6. While the tofu is steaming, in a small saucepan, stir the light soy, sesame oil, vinegar, garlic, ginger, and sugar together over low heat until the sugar is dissolved.
7. Drizzle the warm sauce over the tofu and garnish with the scallions and cilantro.

Stir-Fried Snow Peas

Prep Time: 5 Minutes
Cook Time: 5 Minutes
Serves: 4

Ingredients:

- ¾-pound (about 340g) snow peas or sugar snap peas, strings removed
- 2 peeled fresh ginger slices, each about the size of a quarter
- 2 tablespoons vegetable oil
- Kosher salt

Method:

1. Heat a wok over medium-high heat until a drop of water sizzles and evaporates on contact. Pour in the oil and swirl to coat the base of the wok.
2. Season the oil by adding the ginger slices and a pinch of salt. Allow the ginger to sizzle in the oil for about 30 seconds, swirling gently.
3. Add the snow peas and, using a wok spatula, toss to coat with oil. Stir-fry for 2 to 3 minutes, until bright green and crisp tender.
4. Transfer to a platter and discard the ginger. Serve hot.

Stir-Fried Spinach with Soy Sauce and Garlic

Prep Time: 5 Minutes
Cook Time: 5 Minutes
Serves: 4

Ingredients:

- 8-ounce (about 225g) prewashed baby spinach
- 1 tablespoon light soy sauce
- 2 tablespoons vegetable oil
- 4 garlic cloves, thinly sliced
- 1 teaspoon sugar
- Kosher salt

Method:

1. In a small bowl, stir together the light soy and sugar until the sugar is dissolved and set aside.
2. Heat a wok over medium-high heat until a drop of water sizzles and evaporates on contact. Pour in the oil and swirl to coat the base of the wok.
3. Add the garlic and a pinch of salt and stir-fry, tossing until the garlic is fragrant, about 10 seconds. Using a slotted spoon, remove the garlic from the pan and set aside.
4. Add the spinach to the seasoned oil and stir-fry until the greens are just wilted and bright green.
5. Add the sugar and soy mixture and toss to coat. Return the garlic to the wok and toss to incorporate. Transfer to a dish and serve.

Spicy Stir-Fried Napa Cabbage

Prep Time: 15 Minutes
Cook Time: 10 Minutes
Serves: 4

Ingredients:

- 2 peeled fresh ginger slices, each about the size of a quarter
- 1 head napa cabbage, shredded
- 1 tablespoon light soy sauce

- ½ tablespoon black vinegar
- Freshly ground black pepper
- 2 tablespoons vegetable oil
- 3 or 4 dried chili peppers
- 2 garlic cloves, sliced
- Kosher salt

Method:

1. Heat a wok over medium-high heat until a drop of water sizzles and evaporates on contact. Pour in the oil and swirl to coat the base of the wok.
2. Season the oil by adding the chilies. Allow the chilies to sizzle in the oil for 15 seconds. Add the ginger slices and a pinch of salt. Allow the ginger to sizzle in the oil for about 30 seconds, swirling gently.
3. Toss the garlic in and stir-fry briefly to flavor the oil, about 10 seconds. Do not let the garlic brown or burn.
4. Add the cabbage and stir-fry until it wilts and turns bright green, about 4 minutes.
5. Add the light soy and black vinegar and season with a pinch each of salt and pepper. Toss to coat for another 20 to 30 seconds.
6. Transfer to a platter and discard the ginger. Serve hot.

Stir-Fried Lettuce with Oyster Sauce

Prep Time: 5 Minutes
Cook Time: 10 Minutes
Serves: 4 to 6

Ingredients:

- 1 head iceberg lettuce, rinsed and spun dry, cut into 1-inch-wide pieces
- 1 peeled fresh ginger slice, about the size of a quarter
- 2 garlic cloves, thinly sliced
- 2 tablespoons oyster sauce
- ½ teaspoon sesame oil, for garnish
- 1½ tablespoons vegetable oil
- Kosher salt

Method:

1. Heat a wok over medium-high heat until a drop of water sizzles and evaporates

on contact. Add the vegetable oil and swirl to coat the base of the wok.
2. Season the oil by adding the ginger slice and a pinch of salt. Allow the ginger to sizzle in the oil for about 30 seconds, swirling gently.
3. Add the garlic and stir-fry briefly to flavor the oil, about 10 seconds. Do not let the garlic brown or burn.
4. Add the lettuce and stir-fry until it begins to wilt slightly, 3 to 4 minutes. Drizzle the oyster sauce over the lettuce and quickly toss to coat, another 20 to 30 seconds.
5. Transfer to a platter, discard the ginger, and drizzle with the sesame oil. Serve hot.

Stir-Fried Bamboo Shoots and Broccoli

Prep Time: 5 Minutes
Cook Time: 5 Minutes
Serves: 4

Ingredients:

- 1 (8-ounce (about 225g)) can sliced bamboo shoots, rinsed and drained
- 1 peeled fresh ginger slice, about the size of a quarter
- 2 teaspoons toasted sesame seeds
- 2 tablespoons vegetable oil
- 4 cups broccoli florets
- 2 tablespoons water
- 2 garlic cloves, minced
- 1 tablespoon light soy sauce
- 1 teaspoon sesame oil
- Kosher salt

Method:

1. Heat a wok over medium-high heat until a drop of water sizzles and evaporates on contact. Pour in the vegetable oil and swirl to coat the base of the wok.
2. Season the oil by adding the ginger slice and a pinch of salt. Allow the ginger to sizzle in the oil for about 30 seconds, swirling gently.
3. Add the broccoli and stir-fry for 2 minutes until bright green. Add the water and cover the pan for 2 minutes to steam the broccoli.
4. Remove the cover, add the garlic, and continue stir-frying for 30 seconds. Stir in the bamboo shoots and continue to stir-fry for an additional 30 seconds.
5. Stir in the light soy and sesame oil. Remove the ginger and discard.
6. Serve on a heated platter and garnish with sesame seeds.

Dry-Fried String Beans

Prep Time: 10 Minutes
Cook Time: 15 Minutes
Serves: 4

Ingredients:

- 1 pound (about 454g) of green beans, trimmed, cut in half, and blotted dry
- 1 tablespoon doubanjiang (Chinese chili bean paste)
- 1 tablespoon light soy sauce
- 1 tablespoon minced garlic
- 2 teaspoons sugar
- 1 teaspoon sesame oil
- Kosher salt
- ½ cup vegetable oil

Method:

1. In a small bowl, stir together the light soy, garlic, bean paste, sugar, sesame oil, and a pinch of salt. Set aside.
2. In a wok, heat the vegetable oil over medium-high heat to 375°F (about 190°C), or until it bubbles and sizzles around the end of a wooden spoon.
3. Fry the beans in batches of a couple handfuls at a time (the beans should just cover the oil in a single layer).
4. Gently turn the beans in the oil until they appear wrinkled, 45 seconds to 1 minute, then transfer the green beans to a paper towel-lined plate to drain.
5. Once all the beans have been cooked, carefully transfer the remaining oil to a heatproof container. Use a pair of tongs with a couple of paper towels to wipe and clean out the wok.
6. Return the wok to high heat and add 1 tablespoon of the reserved frying oil. Add the green beans and chili sauce, stir-frying until the sauce comes to a boil and coats the green beans.
7. Transfer the beans to a platter and serve hot.

Stir-Fried Mushrooms and Bok Choy

Prep Time: 10 Minutes
Cook Time: 10 Minutes
Serves: 4

Ingredients:

- ½-pound (about 227g) fresh shiitake mushrooms, stems removed and caps cut into quarters
- 1½-pound (about 680g) baby bok choy, sliced crosswise into 1-inch pieces
- 1 peeled fresh ginger slice, about the size of a quarter
- 2 tablespoons Shaoxing rice wine
- 2 teaspoons light soy sauce
- 2 teaspoons sesame oil
- 3 tablespoons vegetable oil
- 2 garlic cloves, minced
- Kosher salt

Method:

1. Heat a wok over medium-high heat until a drop of water sizzles and evaporates on contact. Pour in the vegetable oil and swirl to coat the base of the wok.
2. Season the oil by adding the ginger slice and a pinch of salt. Allow the ginger to sizzle in the oil for about 30 seconds, swirling gently.
3. Add the mushrooms and stir-fry for 3 to 4 minutes, until they just begin to brown. Add the garlic and stir-fry until fragrant, about 30 seconds more.
4. Add the bok choy and toss with the mushrooms. The wok may appear crowded, but the bok choy will wilt down quickly.
5. Add the rice wine, light soy, and sesame oil. Cook for 3 to 4 minutes, tossing the vegetables constantly until they are tender.
6. Transfer the vegetables to a serving platter, discard the ginger, and serve hot.

Stir-Fried Vegetable Medley

Prep Time: 15 Minutes
Cook Time: 15 Minutes
Serves: 4 to 6

Ingredients:

- 6 fresh shiitake mushrooms, stems removed and caps thinly sliced
- 1 large carrot, peeled and cut diagonally into ¼-inch-thick slices
- 1 peeled fresh ginger slice, about the size of a quarter
- 2 celery ribs, cut diagonally into ¼-inch-thick slices
- ½ white onion, cut into 1-inch pieces
- 1 red bell pepper, cut into 1-inch pieces

- 1 small handful green beans, trimmed
- 3 tablespoons vegetable oil
- 2 garlic cloves, finely minced
- 2 scallions, thinly sliced
- Kosher salt

Method:

1. Heat a wok over medium-high heat until a drop of water sizzles and evaporates on contact. Pour in the oil and swirl to coat the base of the wok.
2. Season the oil by adding the ginger slice and a pinch of salt. Let sizzle in the oil for about 30 seconds, swirling gently.
3. Add the onion, carrot, and celery to the wok and stir-fry, moving the vegetables around in the wok quickly using a spatula.
4. When the vegetables begin to look tender, about 4 minutes, add the mushrooms and continue tossing them in the hot wok.
5. When the mushrooms look soft, add the bell pepper and continue to toss, for about 4 more minutes.
6. When the bell peppers begin to soften, add the green beans and toss until tender, about 3 more minutes. Add the garlic and toss until fragrant.
7. Transfer to a platter, discard the ginger, and garnish with the scallions. Serve hot.

Buddha's Delight

Prep Time: 20 Minutes
Cook Time: 15 Minutes
Serves: 4

Ingredients:

- 1 (8-ounce (about 225g)) can water chestnuts, rinsed and drained
- 2 peeled fresh ginger slices, each about the size of a quarter
- 1 delicata squash, halved, seeded, and cut into bite-size pieces
- Small handful (about ⅓ cup) of dried wood ear mushrooms
- 2 tablespoons Shaoxing rice wine
- 1 cup sugar snap peas, strings removed
- Freshly ground black pepper
- 8 dried shiitake mushrooms
- 2 tablespoons light soy sauce

- 2 teaspoons sugar
- 1 teaspoon sesame oil
- 2 tablespoons vegetable oil
- Kosher salt

Method:

1. Soak both dried mushrooms in separate bowls just covered with hot water until soft, about 20 minutes. Drain and discard the wood ear-soaking liquid. Drain and save ½ cup of the shiitake liquid.
2. To the mushroom liquid add the light soy, sugar, and sesame oil and stir to dissolve the sugar. Set aside.
3. Heat a wok over medium-high heat until a drop of water sizzles and evaporates on contact. Pour in the vegetable oil and swirl to coat the base of the wok.
4. Season the oil by adding the ginger slices and a pinch of salt. Allow the ginger to sizzle in the oil for about 30 seconds, swirling gently.
5. Add the squash and stir-fry, tossing with the seasoned oil for about 3 minutes. Add both mushrooms and the rice wine and continue to stir-fry for 30 seconds.
6. Add the snow peas and water chestnuts, tossing to coat with oil. Add the reserved mushroom seasoning liquid and cover.
7. Continue cooking, stirring occasionally, until the vegetables are just tender, about 5 minutes.
8. Remove the lid and season with salt and pepper to taste. Discard the ginger and serve.

Sesame Asparagus

Prep Time: 5 Minutes
Cook Time: 8 Minutes
Serves: 4

Ingredients:

- 2-pound (about 907g) asparagus, trimmed and cut diagonally into 2-inch-long pieces
- 2 large garlic cloves, coarsely chopped
- 1 tablespoon toasted sesame seeds
- 2 tablespoons light soy sauce
- 1 tablespoon vegetable oil

- 2 tablespoons sesame oil
- 1 teaspoon sugar
- Kosher salt

Method:

1. In a small bowl, stir the light soy and sugar together until the sugar dissolves. Set aside.
2. Heat a wok over medium-high heat until a drop of water sizzles and evaporates on contact.
3. Pour in the vegetable oil and swirl to coat the base of the wok. Add the garlic and stir-fry until fragrant, about 10 seconds.
4. Add the asparagus and stir-fry until crisp-tender, about 4 minutes, seasoning with a small pinch of salt while stir-frying.
5. Add the soy sauce mixture and toss to coat the asparagus, cooking for about 1 minute more.
6. Drizzle the sesame oil over the asparagus and transfer to a serving bowl. Garnish with the sesame seeds and serve hot.

Chinese Broccoli with Oyster Sauce

Prep Time: 5 Minutes
Cook Time: 5 Minutes
Serves: 4

Ingredients:

- 2 bunches Chinese broccoli or broccolini, tough ends trimmed
- 4 peeled fresh ginger slices, each about the size of a quarter
- 2 tablespoons water
- ¼ cup oyster sauce
- 2 teaspoons light soy sauce
- 1 teaspoon sesame oil
- 2 tablespoons vegetable oil
- 4 garlic cloves, peeled
- Kosher salt

Method:

1. In a small bowl, stir together the oyster sauce, light soy, and sesame oil and set

aside.
2. Heat a wok over medium-high heat until a drop of water sizzles and evaporates on contact. Pour in the vegetable oil and swirl to coat the base of the wok.
3. Add the ginger, garlic, and a pinch of salt. Allow the aromatics to sizzle in the oil, swirling gently for about 10 seconds.
4. Add the broccoli and stir, tossing until coated with oil and bright green. Add the water and cover to steam the broccoli for about 3 minutes, or until the stalks can easily be pierced with a knife. Remove the ginger and garlic and discard.
5. Stir in the sauce and toss to coat until hot. Transfer to a serving plate.

Chapter 7: Appetizers and Dim Sum Recipes

Chinese Chicken Salad Cups

Prep Time: 20 Minutes
Cook Time: 8 Minutes
Makes: 15 to 20 Cups

Ingredients:

For the Chicken Cups:

- 4-ounce (about 115g) skinless, boneless chicken tenderloins
- 1 small head of romaine lettuce, shredded
- 3 tablespoons olive oil, divided
- 15 to 20 wonton wrappers
- 1 carrot, julienned
- 2 scallions, chopped
- ¼ cup sliced almonds
- ¼ cup chopped fresh cilantro
- Pepper and salt

For the Salad Dressing:

- 4 tablespoons apple cider vinegar
- 2 tablespoons sesame oil
- 2 tablespoons honey

Method:

1. Season the chicken tenderloins with salt and pepper. In a wok over medium heat, heat 1 tablespoon of olive oil.
2. Add the chicken and sear on both sides until cooked through, about 1 minute per side.
3. Remove the chicken from the wok and chop it finely.
4. Preheat the oven to 375°F (about 190°C).
5. Brush each wonton wrapper on both sides with a thin layer of olive oil. Arrange the wonton wrappers in a regular-size muffin pan to form little cups.
6. Bake the wrappers for 6 minutes. Allow them to cool completely.
7. While the wrappers are baking, make the salad dressing. Combine the apple cider vinegar, sesame oil, and honey in a small bowl, and mix well.
8. in a large bowl, combine the chicken, lettuce, carrot, scallions, almonds, and cilantro with the salad dressing and toss well.
9. Fill each wonton cup with the salad and serve.

Shrimp and Pork Shumai

Prep Time: 20 Minutes
Cook Time: 10 Minutes
Makes: 20 to 25 Shumai

Ingredients:

- ½-pound (about 227g) shrimp, peeled and deveined
- 2 pinches ground white pepper
- 20 to 25-round wonton wrappers
- ½-pound (about 227g) ground pork
- 3 tablespoons sesame oil
- 1 tablespoon cornstarch
- 1 tablespoon soy sauce
- 1 teaspoon grated ginger
- 2 teaspoons Shaoxing wine
- ½ carrot, finely minced
- ½ teaspoon salt

Method:

1. Mince the shrimp by flattening each piece with the side of a knife, then roughly chopping each one.
2. Mix the shrimp and the ground pork.
3. Add the sesame oil, soy sauce, cornstarch, ginger, salt, pepper, and Shaoxing wine to the shrimp and pork. Combine thoroughly.
4. Make an "O" with your thumb and index finger. Place one wonton wrapper on the "O" and gently press it down to create a small cup.
5. Using a teaspoon, fill the wonton cup to the top with some of the pork and shrimp mixture.
6. Use the back of the teaspoon to press the filling into the cup.
7. Line a bamboo steamer with parchment paper liners or napa cabbage leaves.
8. Arrange the shumai on top of the liners or leaves. Top each shumai with a bit of minced carrot.
9. Steam for 10 minutes or until the meat is cooked through.

Shrimp Dumplings

Prep Time: 45 Minutes
Cook Time: 5 Minutes
Makes: 15 to 20 Dumplings

Ingredients:

For the Filling:

- 1 pound (about 454g) peeled and deveined shrimp, roughly chopped
- ¼ cup diced water chestnuts
- 1½ tablespoons sesame oil
- 2 teaspoons soy sauce
- 2 tablespoons cornstarch
- 2 tablespoons finely chopped fresh cilantro (optional)

For the Wrappers:

- 2 tablespoons tapioca flour
- 1¼ cups wheat starch
- 1¼ cups boiling water
- 1 teaspoon peanut oil

Method:

To Make the Filling:

1. in a large bowl, combine the shrimp, sesame oil, soy sauce, water chestnuts, and cornstarch. Add the cilantro (if using). Mix well.
2. Marinate the mixture in the refrigerator for at least 30 minutes.

To Make the Wrappers:

1. in a large bowl, combine the wheat starch and tapioca flour.
2. Slowly pour the boiling water into the flour mixture while stirring, until it starts to form a ball of dough.
3. Cover the bowl with a damp towel and allow the dough to cool down slightly before handling.
4. Cover your palms, a small rolling pin, and a cutting board with a bit of peanut oil to prevent the dough from sticking.
5. Knead the dough for 2 to 3 minutes.
6. Take about a teaspoon of dough and gently roll it into a ball.
7. Roll the dough out into a small pancake, about 3 inches in diameter.

To Make the Dumplings:

1. Set up a bamboo steamer in a wok.
2. Line the steamer with parchment paper liners or napa cabbage leaves.
3. Place about 1 teaspoon of shrimp filling in the middle of a wrapper.
4. Make pleats on one side of the wrapper, then fold the other side of the wrapper toward the pleated side to seal the dumpling.
5. Repeat with the remaining filling and wrappers.
6. Place the dumplings in the bamboo steamer and steam for about 5 minutes or until cooked through.

Savory Scrambled Egg and Crab Lettuce Wraps

Prep Time: 10 Minutes
Cook Time: 10 Minutes
Serves: 4 to 6

Ingredients:

- ½ cup diced water chestnuts
- Pinch ground white pepper
- ½ teaspoon soy sauce
- 2 scallions, chopped
- 3 tablespoons peanut oil
- 1 small onion, thinly sliced
- ¾ cup crab meat
- 1 head lettuce
- 4 eggs, lightly beaten
- Pinch salt
- ¼ cup Basic Sambal (optional)

Method:

1. Wash and separate the lettuce leaves.
2. Chill the lettuce leaves in the refrigerator until just before serving.
3. Put the beaten eggs into a medium bowl.
4. Add the salt, pepper, soy sauce, and scallions to the eggs. Stir gently just to combine.
5. In a wok over medium-high heat, heat the peanut oil.
6. Stir-fry the water chestnuts and onion until the onion is slightly translucent.
7. Add the crabmeat to the wok, then the egg mixture, and let it sit for a moment.
8. When the bottom of the egg is cooked through, flip, and cook on the other side. Using a wok spatula, break up and scramble the egg.
9. Serve with the chilled lettuce leaves and sambal (if using).

Steamed Vegetable Dumplings

Prep Time: 20 Minutes
Cook Time: 10 Minutes
Makes: 15 to 20 Dumplings

Ingredients:

For the Dumplings:

- 2 teaspoons sesame oil, plus 2 teaspoons for brushing
- 5 to 8 garlic chives, cut into 1-inch pieces
- 1-inch piece of ginger, peeled and minced
- 15 to 20-round wonton wrappers
- 2 teaspoons olive oil
- 4 cups shredded cabbage
- 1 carrot, shredded
- 2 scallions, chopped
- 1 tablespoon water
- Pepper and salt

For the Dipping Sauce:

- 1-inch piece of ginger, peeled and finely minced
- 2 tablespoons soy sauce
- 2 teaspoons sesame oil
- 2 teaspoons rice vinegar
- 1 teaspoon chili oil

Method:

1. In a wok over medium heat, heat the olive oil. Add the cabbage, scallions, garlic chives, carrot, and ginger to the wok. Stir-fry for about 1 minute.
2. Add the water to help steam the vegetables. Stir-fry until most of the water has evaporated. Drizzle 2 teaspoons of sesame oil over the vegetables.
3. Season with salt and pepper, and toss. Remove from the heat and set it aside to cool.
4. Place about 1 teaspoon of vegetable mixture in the middle of a wonton wrapper.
5. Dampen the edges of the wonton wrapper with a little water, fold the wrapper in half so that it forms a triangle, and gently press down to seal the edges.
6. Brush the dumplings with a light coating of sesame oil.
7. Line a bamboo steamer with parchment paper liners or napa cabbage leaves.

Arrange the dumplings on top and steam for 8 minutes, or until the wonton wrappers look slightly translucent.
8. While the dumplings are steaming, make the dipping sauce. Combine the soy sauce, sesame oil, rice vinegar, chili oil, and ginger in a small bowl.
9. Serve the dumplings with the dipping sauce.

Chinese Pork Meatballs

Prep Time: 10 Minutes
Cook Time: 10 Minutes
Makes: 20 Meatballs

Ingredients:

- 1 teaspoon five-spice powder
- 2 pinches ground white pepper
- 1-pound (about 454g) ground pork
- 1 tablespoon cornstarch
- 1 teaspoon minced ginger
- 3 garlic cloves, minced
- 2 teaspoons brown sugar
- 2 teaspoons soy sauce
- 3 tablespoons peanut oil

Method:

1. In a large bowl, combine the pork, cornstarch, garlic, brown sugar, soy sauce, ginger, five-spice powder, and pepper, and mix well.
2. Roll 1 heaping tablespoon of pork mixture into a ball and continue until all the pork mixture is used.
3. In a wok over medium heat, heat the peanut oil.
4. Using a wok spatula, spread the oil to coat enough of the wok surface to fry about 10 meatballs at a time.
5. Lower the meatballs into the wok in batches.
6. Cook without moving for about 2 minutes, or until the bottoms are cooked through.
7. Use the spatula to carefully rotate the meatballs to cook on the other sides.
8. Keep rotating the meatballs gently until cooked through.

Cold Sesame Noodles

Prep Time: 10 Minutes
Cook Time: 15 Minutes
Serves: 6 to 8

Ingredients:

- 6-ounce (about 170g) whole-grain spaghetti
- 1-inch piece ginger, peeled and minced
- 2 teaspoons brown sugar or honey
- 2 tablespoons sesame oil, divided
- 2 tablespoons soy sauce
- 1 tablespoon rice vinegar
- 2 teaspoons peanut butter
- 1 carrot, julienned
- 2 scallions, chopped
- 1 tablespoon sesame seeds

Method:

1. Cook the spaghetti according to the package directions for al dente.
2. Rinse the noodles under cold water and toss in 1 tablespoon of sesame oil to prevent the noodles from sticking.
3. in a small bowl, combine the remaining 1 tablespoon of sesame oil, vinegar, brown sugar, soy sauce, and peanut butter, mixing well.
4. Pour the mixture over the noodles then add the carrot, ginger, scallions, and sesame seeds, tossing to combine.
5. Serve chilled.

Chapter 8: The Basics Recipes

Sweet and Sour Sauce

Prep Time: 5 Minutes
Cook Time: 0
Makes: 1 Cup

Ingredients:

- 1½ tablespoons apple cider vinegar
- 5 tablespoons ketchup
- 3 tablespoons water
- 1 tablespoon plum sauce
- 1 tablespoon cornstarch
- 2 teaspoons soy sauce
- 2 teaspoons brown sugar

Method:

1. Combine all the ingredients in a small bowl.
2. Stir well to combine, using the back of the spoon to break up any cornstarch clumps, until the cornstarch has completely dissolved.

Basic Chinese Chicken Stock

Prep Time: 5 Minutes
Cook Time: 3 to 4 Hours
Makes: 8 to 13 Cups

Ingredients:

- 2 large carrots, peeled and quartered
- 1 large yellow onion, peeled and halved
- 2-inch piece ginger, peeled
- 10 to 15 cups water
- 1 whole chicken
- 3 scallions

Method:

1. Put the chicken, carrots, scallions, onion, and ginger in a very large pot.
2. Fill the pot with just enough water to cover the chicken.

3. Simmer on low heat for 3 to 4 hours, partially uncovered.
4. Use an ultra-fine mesh skimmer to remove any froth from the surface, along with any excess oil.
5. Allow the stock to cool slightly then remove the solid ingredients.
6. Run the stock through a fine mesh strainer as you pour it into storage jars or containers.
7. You can refrigerate the stock overnight then simply scoop off the solidified fat. the stock will be kept in the refrigerator for up to 1 week and in the freezer for up to 6 months.

Brown Sauce

Prep Time: 5 Minutes
Cook Time: 0
Makes: 1 Cup

Ingredients:

- 1 cup Basic Chinese Chicken Stock, or store-bought
- 2 tablespoons oyster sauce
- 1 tablespoon soy sauce
- 2 teaspoons cornstarch
- 1 teaspoon brown sugar
- ½ teaspoon sesame oil

Method:

1. Put all the ingredients in a small bowl and stir to combine. Stir well before using.
2. Alternatively, put all the ingredients in a small jar, seal, and gently shake to combine.
3. Shake well before using.

Congee

Prep Time: 5 Minutes
Cook Time: 1 Hour
Serves: 4 to 6

Ingredients:

- 2-inch piece ginger, peeled
- 1 cup short-grain rice
- 6 cups water

Method:

1. First wash the rice. Pour the rice into a medium pot. Rinse the rice by filling the pot halfway with cold tap water, running your fingers through the rice to loosen the starch, then pouring out the murky water. Repeat three or four times, draining as much water as possible. Alternatively, put the rice in a mesh strainer and rinse it under running tap water.
2. Put the rice, ginger, and 6 cups of water in a medium pot.
3. Bring to a boil over high heat, reduce the heat to low, and simmer, partially uncovered, for about 1 hour, stirring occasionally.
4. Serve with your favorite congee toppings (see Serving Tip).

Basic Sambal (Red Chili Sauce)

Prep Time: 5 Minutes
Cook Time: 0
Makes: About ¾ Cup

Ingredients:

- 1 teaspoon freshly squeezed lime juice
- 2 garlic cloves, chopped
- 1 small shallot, thinly sliced
- 6 fresh red chiles
- Pinch salt

Method:

1. Remove the seeds from the chiles, then cut the chiles into thin slices.
2. Put the sliced chiles, garlic, and shallot into a small blender or food processor.
3. Blend for a few seconds or until it forms a paste.
4. Alternatively, use a mortar and pestle to mash the ingredients.
5. Once the mixture is a paste, add the lime juice and salt. Stir to combine.

METRIC CONVERSIONS

1 teaspoon = 5 ml	¾ teaspoon = 3.7 mL
⅔ teaspoon = 3.3 mL	½ teaspoon = 2.5 mL
⅓ teaspoon = 1.6 mL	¼ teaspoon = 1.2 mL
⅛ teaspoon = 0.6 mL	

1 tablespoon = 15mL	¾ tablespoon = 11 mL
⅔ tablespoon = 10 mL	½ tablespoon = 7.4 mL
⅓ tablespoon = 5 mL	¼ tablespoon = 3.7 mL
⅛ tablespoon = 1.8 mL	

1 cup = 237 mL	¾ cup = 177 mL
⅔ cup = 158 mL	½ cup = 118 mL
⅓ cup = 79 mL	¼ cup = 59 mL
⅛ cup = 30 mL	

Printed in Great Britain
by Amazon